COMPREHENSIVE RESEARCH
AND STUDY GUIDE

BLOOM'S
MAJOR
SHORT STORY
WRITERS

Isaac
Babel

EDITED AND WITH AN
INTRODUCTION BY HAROLD BLOOM

CURRENTLY AVAILABLE

COMPREHENSIVE RESEARCH
AND STUDY GUIDE

BLOOM'S
MAJOR
SHORT
STORY
WRITERS

Isaac
Babel

CHELSEA HOUSE
PUBLISHERS
A Haights Cross Communications Company
Philadelphia

EDITED AND WITH AN INTRODUCTION BY HAROLD BLOOM

First Printing
1 3 5 7 9 8 6 4 2

Library of Congress Cataloging-in-Publication Data

Isaac Babel / edited and with an introduction by Harold Bloom.
    p. cm — (Bloom's Major Short Story Writers)
Includes bibliographical references and index.
    ISBN 0-7910-7590-7
    1. Babel§, I. (Isaak), 1894–1941—Criticism and interpretation. 2.
Babel§, I. (Isaak), 1994–1941—Examinations—Study guides. I. Bloom,
Harold. II. Title. III. Series.
    PG3476.B2Z716 2003
    891.73'41—dc22
                                                        2003016871

Chelsea House Publishers
1974 Sproul Road, Suite 400
Broomall, PA 19008-0914

www.chelseahouse.com

Contributing Editor: Jenn McKee

Cover design by Keith Trego

Layout by EJB Publishing Services

CONTENTS

USER'S GUIDE

This volume is designed to present biographical, critical, and bibliographical information on the author and the author's best-known or most important short stories. Following Harold Bloom's editor's note and introduction is a concise biography of the author that discusses major life events and important literary accomplishments. A critical analysis of each story follows, tracing significant themes, patterns, and motifs in the work. An annotated list of characters supplies brief information on the main characters in each story.

A selection of critical extracts, derived from previously published material, follows each thematic analysis. In most cases, these extracts represent the best analysis available from a number of leading critics. Because these extracts are derived from previously published material, they will include the original notations and references when available. Each extract is cited, and readers are encouraged to use the original publications as they continue their research. A bibliography of the author's writings, a list of additional books and articles on the author and their work, and an index of themes and ideas conclude the volume.

As with any study guide, this volume is designed as a supplement to the works being discussed, and is in no way intended as a replacement for those works. The reader is advised to read the text prior to using this study guide, and to keep it accessible for quick reference.

ABOUT THE EDITOR

Harold Bloom is Sterling Professor of the Humanities at Yale University and Henry W. and Albert A. Berg Professor of English at the New York University Graduate School. He is the author of over 20 books, and the editor of more than 30 anthologies of literary criticism.

Professor Bloom's works include *Shelley's Mythmaking* (1959), *The Visionary Company* (1961), *Blake's Apocalypse* (1963), *Yeats* (1970), *A Map of Misreading* (1975), *Kabbalah and Criticism* (1975), *Agon: Toward a Theory of Revisionism* (1982), *The American Religion* (1992), *The Western Canon* (1994), and *Omens of Millennium: The Gnosis of Angels, Dreams, and Resurrection* (1996). *The Anxiety of Influence* (1973) sets forth Professor Bloom's provocative theory of the literary relationships between the great writers and their predecessors. His most recent books include *Shakespeare: The Invention of the Human*, a 1998 National Book Award finalist, *How to Read and Why* (2000), and *Genius: A Mosaic of One Hundred Exemplary Creative Minds* (2002).

Professor Bloom earned his Ph.D. from Yale University in 1955 and has served on the Yale faculty since then. He is a 1985 MacArthur Foundation Award recipient and served as the Charles Eliot Norton Professor of Poetry at Harvard University in 1987–88. In 1999 he was awarded the prestigious American Academy of Arts and Letters Gold Medal for Criticism. Professor Bloom is the editor of several other Chelsea House series in literary criticism, including BLOOM'S MAJOR SHORT STORY WRITERS, BLOOM'S MAJOR NOVELISTS, BLOOM'S MAJOR DRAMATISTS, BLOOM'S MODERN CRITICAL INTERPRETATIONS, BLOOM'S MODERN CRITICAL VIEWS, and BLOOM'S BIOCRITIQUES.

EDITOR'S NOTE

My Introduction disagrees with Lionel Trilling's notion that Babel's stance towards the Cossacks in any way celebrates their brutal vitality. I then proceed to Babel's actual celebration of the Jewish Odessa of his childhood.

As there are twenty valuable critical views on four superb stories excerpted here, I will comment upon only a few that I find particularly illuminating.

Efraim Sicher centers upon Babel's ambivalences in "My First Goose," while "The Story of My Dovecote" is analyzed by Patricia Carden as Babel's education in regard to anti-Semitic violence.

"The Awakening" is interpreted by James E. Falen as Babel's resolution to integrate the realms of art and of experience.

The great, tragic story, "Guy de Maupassant," is worthy of the attention of the great scholar-critic, Victor Erlich, who traces in it the profound, prophetic parable of Babel's own martyrdom to art, the highest art that he felt compelled to create even in Stalin's Russia.

Harold Bloom

I

"If you need my life you may have it, but all make mistakes, God included. A terrible mistake has been made, Aunt Pesya. But wasn't it a mistake on the part of God to settle Jews in Russia, for there to be tormented worse than in Hell? How would it hurt if the Jews lived in Switzerland, where they would be surrounded by first-class lakes, mountain air, and nothing but Frenchies? All make mistakes, not God excepted."
—"How It Was Done in Odessa"

Benya Krik, Babel's outrageously insouciant gangster boss of Jewish Odessa, utters this defense to the bereaved Aunt Pesya, whose wretched son has just been slain by one of Benya's hoods in an exuberant error. The Jewish presence in Russia, then and now, is one of God's exuberant errors, and is both the subject and the rhetorical stance of Babel's extraordinary art as a writer of short stories. Babel's precursors were Gogol and Guy de Maupassant (and Maupassant's literary "father," Flaubert) but repeated rereadings of Babel's best stories tend to show a very different and older tradition also at work. Babel's expressionist and economical art has unmistakably Jewish literary antecedents. The late Lionel Trilling undoubtedly was the most distinguished critic to write about Babel in English, but he underestimated the Jewish element in Babel, and perhaps introduced a perspective into Babel's stories that the stories themselves repudiate.

Babel was murdered in a Stalinist purge before he was forty-seven. His work was not officially forbidden in the former Soviet Union, and he was legally cleared of all charges in 1956, fifteen years after his death. Yet there are few editions of his stories, and little Soviet criticism is devoted to them. Presumably Babel's erotic intensity did not please cultural bureaucrats, and so overtly

Jewish a writer, in mode and in substance, was an uncomfortable shadow in a country where teaching Hebrew was a legal offence. Anyone who believes that Babel's world is wholly lost ought to wander some Friday evening through "Little Odessa," as Brighton Beach in Brooklyn has been called. Benya Krik's descendents are alive and well, a little too well, in Little Odessa. Babel is the storyteller of Jewish Odessa, the city also of Vladimir Jabotinsky, founder of the Zionist Right, teacher and inspirer of Menachem Begin and the Irgun Zvai Leumi. The Odessa of Babel was a great center of Jewish literary culture, the city also of the Hebrew poet Bialik, and of the Yiddish writer Mendele Mocher Sforim. Like Bialik and Sforim, Babel writes out of the context of Yiddish-speaking Odessa, though Babel wrote in Russian.

Trilling ought to have had second thoughts about his characterization of Babel's self-representation in *Red Cavalry* as "a Jew riding as a Cossack and trying to come to terms with the Cossack ethos." Lyutov, Babel's surrogate, is trying to survive, but hardly at the cost of coming to terms with the Cossack ethos, terms that Tolstoy in one of his modes accepted. On the contrary, Babel's Cossacks are not Tolstoyan noble savages, but are precisely the Cossacks as the Jews saw them: subhuman and bestial, mindlessly violent. Trilling imported something of his own nostalgia for the primitive into Babel, with curious results:

> Babel's view of the Cossack was more consonant with that of Tolstoy than with the traditional view of his own people. For him the Cossack was indeed the noble savage, all too savage, not often noble, yet having in his savagery some quality that might raise strange questions in a Jewish mind.

But those questions certainly are not raised in Babel's mind, the mind of the Odessa Jew, with a perpetually glowing awareness of "how it was done in Odessa." That awareness informs his two very different ways of representing violence, ways that urgently need to be contrasted when we reflect on Babel's stories. This is one way:

Then Benya took steps. They came in the night, nine of them, bearing long poles in their hands. The poles were wrapped about with pitch-dipped tow. Nine flaming stars flared in Eichbaum's cattle yard. Benya beat the locks from the door of the cowshed and began to lead the cows out one by one. Each was received by a lad with a knife. He would overturn the cow with one blow of the fist and plunge his knife into her heart. On the blood-flooded ground the torches bloomed like roses of fire. Shots rang out. With these shots Benya scared away the dairymaids who had come hurrying to the cowshed. After him other bandits began firing in the air. (If you don't fire in the air you may kill someone.) And now, when the sixth cow had fallen, mooing her death-moo, at the feet of the King, into the courtyard in his underclothes galloped Eichbaum.

("The King")

And meantime misfortune lurked beneath the window like a pauper at daybreak. Misfortune broke noisily into the office. And though on this occasion it bore the shape of the Jew Savka Butsis, this misfortune was as drunk as a water-carrier.

"Ho-hoo-ho," cried the Jew Savka, "forgive me, Benya, I'm late." And he started stamping his feet and waving his arms about. Then he fired, and the bullet landed in Muginstein's belly.

Are words necessary? A man was, and is no more. A harmless bachelor was living his life like a bird on a bough, and had to meet a nonsensical end. There came a Jew looking like a sailor and took a potshot not at some clay pipe or dolly but at a live man. Are words necessary?

("How It Was Done in Odessa")

This is the other way, the violence of the Cossack and not of the Odessa Jew:

But I wasn't going to shoot him. I didn't owe him a shot anyway, so I only dragged him upstairs into the parlor. There in the parlor was Nadezhda Vasilyevna clean off her head, with a drawn saber in her hand, walking about and looking at herself in the glass. And when I dragged Nikitinsky into the parlor she ran and sat down in the armchair. She had a velvet crown on trimmed with feathers. She sat in the armchair very brisk and alert and saluted me with the saber. Then I stamped on my master Nikitinsky, trampled on him for an hour or maybe more. And in that time I got to know life through and through. With shooting—I'll put it this way—with shooting you only get rid of a chap. Shooting's letting him off, and too damn easy for yourself. With shooting you'll never get at the soul, to where it is in a fellow and how it shows itself. But I don't spare myself, and I've more than once trampled an enemy for over an hour. You see, I want to get to know what life really is, what life's like down our way.

("The Life and Adventures of Matthew Pavlichenko")

Notices were already posted up announcing that Divisional Commissar Vinogradov would lecture that evening on the second congress of the Comintern. Right under my window some Cossacks were trying to shoot an old silvery-bearded Jew for spying. The old man was uttering piercing screams and struggling to get away. Then Kudrya of the machine gun section took hold of his head and tucked it under his arm. The Jew stopped screaming and straddled his legs. Kudrya drew out his dagger with his right hand and carefully, without splashing himself, cut the old man's throat. Then he knocked at the closed window.

"Anyone who cares may come and fetch him," he said. "You're free to do so."

("Berestechko")

The first way is violence stylized as in a child's vision: "On the blood-flooded ground the torches bloomed like roses of fire," and "There came a Jew looking like a sailor and took a potshot." The second way is highly stylized also, but as in the vision of a historical Jewish irony: "With shooting you'll never get at the soul, to where it is in a fellow and how it shows itself," and "carefully, without splashing himself, cut the old man's throat." When Babel represents the violence of the Jewish gangs of the Moldavanka, he colors it as he renders Benya Krik's wardrobe: "He wore an orange suit, beneath his cuff gleamed a bracelet set with diamonds," and "aristocrats of the Moldavanka, they were tightly encased in raspberry waistcoats. Russet jackets clasped their shoulders, and on their fleshy feet the azure leather cracked." But Babel's representation of "the training of the famous Kniga, the headstrong Pavlichenko, and the captivating Savitsky," is quite another matter. The irony, ferociously subtle, is built up by nuances until the supposed nostalgia for the virtues of murderous barbarity becomes a kind of monstrous Jewish in-joke. General Budenny's fury, when he denounced *Red Cavalry* as a slander upon his Cossacks, was not wholly misplaced.

II

Whatever the phrase "a Jewish writer" may be taken to mean, any meaning assigned to it that excludes Babel will not be very interesting. Maurice Friedberg, the authority on Babel's relation to Yiddish folklore and literature, rather strangely remarks of him that: "A leftist, Russian, Jewish intellectual, particularly one strongly influenced by the adamant anti-clericalism of the French Left, could hardly be expected to return to the fold of organized religion." That Babel did not trust in the Covenant, in any strict sense, is palpably true, but the nuances of Jewish spirituality, at any time, are notoriously difficult to ascertain.

Babel's irony is so pervasive that sometimes it does threaten to turn into the irony of irony, and yet sometimes it barely masks Babel's true nostalgia, which is not exactly for the primitive. Gedali, Babel's "tiny, lonely visionary in a black top hat, carrying a big prayerbook under his arm," may be as ironic a figure as the "captivating" Savitsky, whose "long legs were like girls sheathed to the neck in shining riding boots," but the two ironies are as different as the two visions of violence, and can be conveyed again by a textual clash:

> We all of us seated ourselves side by side—possessed, liars, and idlers. In a corner, some broad-shouldered Jews who resembled fishermen and apostles were moaning over their prayerbooks. Gedali, in his green frock coat down to the ground, was dozing by the wall like a little bright bird. And suddenly I caught sight of a youth behind him, a youth with the face of Spinoza, with Spinoza's powerful brow and the wan face of a nun. He was smoking, shuddering like a recaptured prisoner brought back to his cell. The ragged Reb Mordecai crept up to him from behind, snatched the cigarette from his mouth, and ran away to me.
> "That's Elijah, the Rabbi's son," he declared hoarsely, bringing his bloodshot eyelids close to my face. "That's the cursed son, the last son, the unruly son."
>
> ("The Rabbi")

> His things were strewn about pell-mell—mandates of the propagandist and notebooks of the Jewish poet, the portraits of Lenin and Maimonides lay side by side, the knotted iron of Lenin's skull beside the dull silk of the portraits of Maimonides. A lock of woman's hair lay in a book, the Resolutions of the Party's Sixth Congress, and the margins of Communist leaflets were crowded with crooked lines of ancient Hebrew verse. They fell upon me in a mean and depressing rain—pages of the Song of Songs and revolver cartridges. The dreary rain of sunset washed the dust in my hair, and I said to the boy who was dying on a wretched mattress in the corner:
> "One Friday evening four months ago, Gedali the old-clothes-man took me to see your father, Rabbi Motale. But you didn't belong to the Party at that time, Bratslavsky."
>
> ("The Rabbi's Son")

And I don't mind telling you straight that I threw that female citizen down the railway embankment while the train was still going. But she, being big and broad, just sat there awhile, flapped her skirts, and started to go her vile way. And seeing that scatheless woman going along like that and Russia around her like I don't know what, and the peasant fields without an ear of corn and the outraged girls and the comrades lots of which go to the front but few return, I had a mind to jump out of the truck and put an end to my life or else put an end to hers. But the Cossacks took pity on me and said:

"Give it her with your rifle."

So I took my faithful rifle off the wall and washed away that stain from the face of the worker's land and the republic.

("Salt")

The pathos of Elijah the Rabbi's son is rendered bearable by a purely defensive irony, the irony of incommensurate juxtapositions, of Communist leaflets and the Hebrew Song of Songs. Irony in "Salt" dissolves all pathos, and defends Babel, not from his own affections and identifications, but from Cossack bestiality. It cannot be that Babel did not understand his own cultural affections. His first mode of irony is altogether biblical, and is neither the irony of saying one thing while meaning another, as in "Salt," nor the irony that contrasts expectation and fulfillment, for no expectations remain in "The Rabbi" and "The Rabbi's Son." Babel writes the irony of the Covenant, the incommensurateness of the Chooser and the chosen. That irony is no less Jewish than the allegory of "Salt," but its Jewishness is far more archaic.

III

The best of Babel's stories are neither in *Red Cavalry* nor in the *Tales of Odessa*, though those are my personal favorites. Babel's best work is in "The Story of My Dovecot," "First Love," "In the Basement," "Awakening," "Guy de Maupassant," "Di Grasso"—

all tales of Odessa, but with the difference that they are tales of Babel himself, and not of Benya Krik. But if a single story has in it the center of Babel's achievement, it is the extraordinary, outrageous, and ultimately plangent "The End of the Old Folk's Home." Restraining himself from overtly celebrating the raffish inmates of the poorhouse by the Second Jewish Cemetery in Odessa, Babel nevertheless portrays this motley group of old men and women with a gusto and exuberance that make them the peers of Benya Krik the gangster. Gravediggers, cantors, washers of corpses, they live by their wits and unscrupulousness in hiring out their single oak coffin with a pall and silver tassles, recycling it through endless burials.

Alas, the Bolsheviks use the coffin to bury one Hersch Lugovoy with full military honors, pushing away the old men when they attempt to turn the coffin on its side so as to roll out the flag-draped corpse of the heroic and faithful Jewish Bolshevik. The rest of the story, an astonishing mixture of Dickensian pathos and Gogolian humor, portrays the doomed but still vital antics of the old folk in their final days before they are evicted from the poorhouse. With the expulsion itself, Babel achieves his finest conclusion:

> The tall horse bore him and the manager of the department of public welfare townwards. On their way they passed the old folk who had been evicted from the poorhouse. Limping, bowed beneath their bundles, they plodded along in silence. Bluff Red Army men were keeping them in line. The little carts of paralytics squeaked; the whistle of asthma, a humble gurgling issued from the breasts of retired cantors, jesters at weddings, cooks at circumcisions, and ancient shop-assistants.
>
> The sun stood high in the sky, and its rays scorched the rags trailing along the road. Their path lay along a cheerless, parched and stony highway, past huts of rammed clay, past stone-cluttered fields, past houses torn open by shells, past the Plague Mound. An unspeakably sorrowful road once led from the cemetery to Odessa.
>
> ("The End of the Old Folk's Home")

The troping of "road" for the unspeakably sorrowful procession itself is characteristic of Babel. As for the squeaking, whistling, and "humble gurgling," it is the funeral music by which Babel implicitly laments the loss of a desperate vitalism in the old folk, roisterers who in a sense are coffin-robbers, but never grave-robbers. These aged scamps are Babel's heroes and heroines, even as the Bolshevik bureaucrats and brutal Cossacks are not. Presumably Babel was another victim of Stalin's virulent anti-Semitism, but his best stories transcend his victimization. They give nothing away to the anti-Semites, nothing away even to Stalin himself. We hear in them finally a voice masterly in its ironies, yes, but also a voice of comic celebration eternally commemorating "the image of the stout and jovial Jews of the South, bubbling like cheap wine." Benya Krik's heroic funeral for the poor clerk killed by mistake is a superb exemplification of Babel's art at its most joyous:

And the funeral was performed the next morning. Ask the cemetery beggars about that funeral. Ask the shamessim from the synagogue of the dealers in kosher poultry about it, or the old women from the Second Almshouse. Odessa had never before seen such a funeral, the world will never see such a funeral. On that day the cops wore cotton gloves. In the synagogues, decked with greenstuff and wide open, the electric lights were burning. Black plumes swayed on the white horses harnessed to the hearse. A choir of sixty headed the cortege: a choir of boys, but they sang with the voice of women. The Elders of the synagogue of the dealers in kosher poultry helped Aunt Pesya along. Behind the elders walked members of the Association of Jewish Shop Assistants, and behind the Jewish Shop Assistants walked the lawyers, doctors of medicine, and certified midwives. On one side of Aunt Pesya were the women who trade in poultry on the Old Market, and on the other side, draped in orange shawls, were the honorary dairymaids from Bugayevka. They stamped their feet like gendarmes parading on a holiday. From their wide hips wafted the odors of the sea and of milk. And behind them all plodded Ruvim Tartakovsky's employees. There were a hundred of them, or two hundred, or two thousand. They wore black frock coats with silk lapels and new shoes that squeaked like sacked suckling-pigs.

("How It Was Done in Odessa")

Those orange-shawled "honorary dairymaids," stamping their feet like gendarmes on parade while "from their wide hips wafted the odors of the sea and of milk," are Babel's true Muses. The entire paragraph becomes a phantasmagoria, a visionary evocation of a Jewish child's delight in the muscular exuberance of the Odessa mob. Babel's pragmatic sorrow was in his political context. His joy, fantastic and infectious, was in his nostalgia for his own childhood, and for the archaic and celebratory force of the Jewish tradition that claimed him, after all, for its own.

Isaac Babel

For many years, the facts of Isaac Babel's short life were cloudy, and the situation was made far worse by the propensity of the author himself to report certain falsehoods as truth. (Babel even went so far as to publish a short piece titled "Autobiography," which featured several untrue statements about his life and experiences.) However, despite this obstacle, scholars have recently been able to glean the basic facts about the gifted author's life, up to and including his government-ordered death.

Isaac Emmanuelovich Babel was born on June 30, 1894 in a poor section of Odessa, a vibrant Ukrainian city with a large Jewish community. Babel's father, Emmanuil, sold agricultural machinery, and soon after Isaac's birth, he moved his son and his wife, Feiga, to Nikolayev, a Black Sea port town that lies one hundred fifty kilometers from Odessa. There, Babel studied languages—English, French, German, and Hebrew—and in 1899, his sister Meriam was born.

A few years later, in 1905, Czar Nicholas II declared Russia a monarchy through a new constitution, and this action fueled pogroms in Southern Russia, including the town of Nikolayev; Babel likely witnessed these riots, but he and his family survived, unharmed. In 1906, Babel's family moved back to Odessa, where he attended school and began writing stories. But in 1911— similar to the narrator's plight in Babel's story, "The Story of My Dovecote"—the University of Odessa rejected Babel because of tight restrictions on the number of Jews who could enroll. For this reason, Babel instead enrolled in the Institute of Finance and Business Studies in Kiev to study economics, thinking he might follow in his father's footsteps; while there, Babel met Eugenia Gronfein, the woman he would later marry.

In 1913, Babel enjoyed his first publication—the story "Old Shloime"—but one year later, World War I broke out. This caused Babel's school to evacuate to Saratov, where the writer finished his studies and graduated. In 1916, he moved to Petrograd and lived comfortably with a Jewish engineer's family, writing stories for local publications, including Maxim Gorky's *Letopis* (*Chronicle*). His relationship with Gorky evolved into a friendship, and Gorky became Babel's lifelong, literary mentor.

In 1917, Babel volunteered for military service, and after the October Revolution definitively put the Bolsheviks in power that same year, Babel returned to Odessa and worked briefly as a translator for Petrograd's Cheka (the Soviet secret police). During this unusually free time of transition, Babel contributed regularly to Gorky's anti-Leninist newspaper in 1918, until the government shut it down.

In 1919, Babel married Eugenia Gronfein, but left her alone for months the following year in order to ride alongside a group of Cossack soldiers as a war correspondent. At this time, the Cossack army fought the White Army, who wished to restore a monarchy to Russia, and led an unsuccessful campaign to spread communism into Poland. Babel accompanied them for four months—June through September—but he eventually contracted typhus and returned to Odessa.

The civil war, fought by the White and Red armies, finally ended in 1921, and at that time, Babel did editing work for a publishing house in Odessa while also writing and contributing stories to various periodicals. In 1923 and 1924, nearly all of the Odessa stories—which featured humorous portrayals of the Jewish underworld, including colorful characters like gangsters, whores, small merchants, brokers, rabbis, saloon keepers, and entrepreneurs—were published individually; additionally, Babel began working on a group of stories based on his experiences with the Cossacks, a collection that would become *Red Cavalry*. In 1924 (after Lenin died and Stalin rose to power), Babel's sister Meriam emigrated to Belgium, and Babel's wife followed Meriam's lead in 1925, establishing a home for herself in Paris. Babel, however, temporarily separating from his wife, had no wish to permanently leave the Soviet Union.

In 1926, both *Red Cavalry* and *The Story of My Dovecote*—a compilation which featured Babel's autobiographical stories about his childhood—were released for the first time as collections. Babel also drafted a play called *Sunset* and worked on a screenplay for *Benya Krik* during this year, while his mistress, the actress Tamara Kashirna, gave birth to Babel's son, Mikhail. (The child was later adopted by the actress's future husband, a writer named Vsevolod Ivanov.) In spite of the birth of his first child, Babel traveled to Paris in 1927 and remained there with his wife Eugenia for over a year. During his stay, he wrote more childhood stories, and just before leaving, Babel's wife became pregnant, giving birth to Babel's daughter, Nathalie, in July of 1929. Aside from Babel's biological productivity, however, many Russian critics began to voice concerns about Babel's low literary productivity. They publicly reprimanded Babel's apparent "silence" in the face of an increasingly polarized ideological schism; for in the climate of a police state, silence implied subversive thought and, potentially, subversive actions.

Trotsky was exiled from Russia at the start of 1929, intensifying Stalin's already anxious, paranoid watchfulness, and Babel set out, like many Soviet writers of the time, to explore the industrial heartland, learning and writing about collectivization in the Ukraine. After Babel concluded his travels, he lived near Moscow, and while he didn't publish anything notable about the collectivization he witnessed, he published, in 1932, some of his most famous stories, including "The Awakening" and "Guy de Maupassant." (In this year, he also met Antonina Nikolaevna Pirozhkova, an engineer who would become his "unofficial" second wife in Russia.) Near the end of 1932, Babel pleaded his way out of the country in order to see Eugenia and Nathalie in Paris, and he stayed until August 1933. The following year, at the First Congress of Soviet Writers, Babel obliquely criticized Stalin's government and deemed himself the "master of silence."

This caused him, the following year, to be denied inclusion in the Anti-Fascist International Congress of Writers for the Defense of Culture and Peace, a gathering scheduled to take place in Paris. André Gide and André Malraux, however, strongly protested this decision, insisting that not only Babel, but also Boris Pasternak (most famous for his novel, *Doctor Zhivago*), must be included. For this reason, the government finally allowed Babel to go. While in Paris, he visited his wife and daughter, traveling to Brussels with them to see his sister and mother. He wished to bring everyone back to the Soviet Union with him, but he was unsuccessful in his arguments, and he returned to the Soviet Union alone in August, 1935. Babel traveled with Antonina Pirozhkova for a time, and upon their return to Moscow, they established a home together.

In 1937, Antonina gave birth to Lydia, Babel's daughter, while trials of military and political figures proliferated in an ongoing "purge." In 1939, Babel moved to a writer's colony to work on a new collection of stories, but on May 15, he was arrested by the NKVD (a precursor of the KGB), and all his documents, including works-in-progess, were confiscated, never to be found again. On January 26, 1940, Babel, after a twenty-minute military tribunal, was found guilty of spying for France and Austria, as well as for conspiracy. He was sentenced to death and was shot early the next morning.

Babel's assassination remained a secret for years. In 1948, for example, rumors circulated that Babel would soon be released from a work camp, where he was a prisoner; Antonina Pirozhkova herself held out hope that Babel was still alive for more than a decade after his death. Only after Stalin's death in 1953 did the truth come out, and Babel was publicly exonerated the next year.

In spite of now knowing the basic facts of Isaac Babel's life, critics and scholars have nonetheless noted the lingering elusive quality of the writer. In addition to having a relatively small volume of published work, Babel bizarrely seemed also able to achieve mystery by way of his seldom-photographed appearance. Critic Lionel Trilling wrote, "I have seen three pictures of Babel, and it is a puzzle to know how he was supposed to look." This, while confirming daughter Nathalie Babel's remark that her father "loved to confuse and mystify people," echoes the atmosphere evoked in much of Babel's work—for indeed, the yearning search to define one's sense of self and identity, and the inherent, endless difficulties of this task, make up the core of his work, and make it resonate with readers still.

"My First Goose"

Part of Babel's *Red Cavalry* collection, critics have often isolated "My First Goose" as representative of the themes and complexities that haunt the short story collection as a whole—specifically, Babel's complicated sense of self in regard to his Jewishness. The story's title would seem to suggest a positive experience, even perhaps a holiday celebration, during childhood. As is common with Babel, however, the title deceptively raises the reader's expectations in precisely the wrong way, so that the austerity and violence that follow cut all the more sharply.

The story opens with the bespectacled, Jewish, intellectual narrator approaching Savitsky, the Red Cavalry's physically imposing Cossack leader. The narrator's evocation of Savitsky seems both mythologically hyperbolic and erotic, particularly when the narrator notes how he split "the hut in two like a banner splitting the sky," and how the man's "long legs looked like two girls wedged to their shoulders in riding boots." The earthy, large Cossack is a masculine, strong, sexual being, while the narrator's timidity in Savitsky's presence posits that as a Jewish man, he views himself as Savitsky's opposite: an effeminate, weak, non-sexual being.

Savitsky smiles at the narrator, smacks the table with his whip, then finishes writing an order for another officer, Chesnokov, to approach and destroy the enemy. Savitsky notes that if Chesnokov fails, Savitsky himself will gun him down. He signs the order, tosses it to orderlies, and turns his attention to the narrator, who gives him documents regarding his assignment. Savitsky barks orders about granting the narrator "amusements," rather than "provisions," specifically noting that he should receive all but "those of the frontal kind." In this way, not only does Savitsky's size seem to emasculate the narrator's sense of himself, but his teasing does as well.

Savitsky asks the narrator whether he can read and write. The narrator, envying Savitsky's youth, tells him that he graduated with a law degree from the University of Petersburg, which causes Savitsky to burst out laughing. He mocks the narrator—calling him a "powder puff," mocking his glasses, telling him that no one wants him there—and insinuates that he's not tough enough to live among the Cossack soldiers. (Here, Jewishness is reiterated as a source of shame—Jewish men are "lesser" men by way of their valuing of intellect, their sensibilities, and their small physical size.) The narrator simply answers that he thinks he can do what's required, and goes to the village with the quartermaster to look for lodgings.

The quartermaster, carrying the narrator's suitcase, emphasizing the distinctions between the Cossacks and the Jews once again, takes him to a hut and tells him that while a prejudice about intellectuals is prevalent among the men, "ruining" a woman raises one's social capital. The quartermaster comes close to the narrator, but then lunges away, reaching a group of Cossacks in a courtyard, who are shaving each other while sitting on bales of hay. The quartermaster addresses them, telling them that by Savitsky's orders, they are "to accept this man," the narrator, among them, and then jokes that they are not to meddle with him, since he has "suffered on the fields of learning!" The quartermaster leaves abruptly, and the narrator salutes, only to watch a Cossack throw the narrator's suitcase out into the street. A young soldier then shows his backside to the narrator, making vulgar noises. The narrator gathers up the manuscripts and ragged clothes that fall from the suitcase, then carries them to the other end of the yard. He notes that a pot of boiling pork stands in front of the hut, and this image makes him homesick. He covers his suitcase with hay, making a pillow, and lies down to read a speech of Lenin's in Pravda. The Cossacks step over his legs, and the young soldier keeps teasing him, so that he can't enjoy the speech and finally puts the newspaper away. He approaches the hut's mistress (or "landlady"), who sits on her porch spinning yarn (notably, the literal image of storytelling, which aligns her immediately with the narrator).

He tells her he needs food, to which she says, "All of this makes me want to hang myself." This angers the narrator, who pushes her and curses. He turns and spots a saber, as well as a "haughty goose" grooming its feathers in the yard. (Readers should note that it isn't even his "saber," which may be interpreted as a phallic symbol; significantly, the narrator must take a Cossack's sword in order to commit even his small-scale act of violence.) The narrator catches the goose and crushes its head under his boot, its neck in dung. He curses at the woman again, pokes the saber at the goose, and demands that she roast it for him. Silently, she carries the bird in her apron to the kitchen, but before she shuts the door behind her, she says again, "Comrade ... This makes me want to hang myself." Critics have noted that like the narrator, the woman wears spectacles, aligning her with him again, and thus showing his anger and actions toward her to be an externalization of his own self-loathing.

Conversely, the violence of the act calls to mind the tension surrounding masculinity and sexuality in the story, particularly when readers note the detail about the goose's white neck, a particularly feminine image, lying in dung. Thus, the narrator performs a somewhat cartoonish, silly version of what the quartermaster suggested: he commits a kind of rape, on a small scale, against a defenseless animal in order to gain acceptance into the group of Cossacks. This would appear, in a way, to belittle the Jewish man once again—even when he commits violence, it's of the no-risk, nobody-gets-hurt variety, while the Cossacks, whom he admires, kill human beings regularly. The narrator's act is that of a wanna-be; a sycophant.

Nonetheless, the "rape" works to its intended effect. At first, the Cossacks gather around their pot in the yard, still as stones, not seeing the goose. But one soon remarks that the narrator will fit into a place at the fire and winks. The narrator cleans off the saber then wanders out from, and back into, the courtyard, "feeling anguished." Thus, contrary to the nourishment we might expect from the goose in the story's title, the fowl acts, in fact, to emotionally disturb and drain the narrator.

Soon, the oldest Cossack calls out to the narrator and suggests that he have some soup with them until the goose is ready, offering an extra spoon from his boot. The narrator has soup and pork with them, thus sharing in a ritual of community, and the young soldier who previously made vulgar noises now makes room in the circle for the narrator and asks about what is in the newspaper. The narrator tells them about Lenin's speech, then reads it to them. The squadron commander, Surovkov, remarks on how Lenin can pick out what's true from "the pile of rubbish," and the men soon sleep in the hayloft, six together, "our legs tangled, under the holes in the roof which let in the stars." But in contrast to this warm, somewhat erotic image, the story concludes with the narrator noting, "I dreamed and saw women in my dreams, and only my heart, crimson with murder, screeched and bled." This image echoes words used to evoke the goose's killing, aligning the narrator with the brutalized goose. Thus, by killing the bird—a scenario which appears repeatedly in Babel's stories—the narrator has killed something important within himself: his humanity, his self-respect, and his identity as a Jewish man.

"My First Goose"

The narrator (or **Liutov**, as indicated by other stories in *Red Cavalry*) is a Russian Jew, sent to work with the Cossacks as they attempt (unsuccessfully) to conquer Poland for the Soviet Union. Awed by the Cossacks' strength, toughness, and size, he tries desperately to prove their prejudices about him, as an intellectual and as a Jew, wrong. But rather than raping a woman, as the quartermaster suggests, he harasses an old woman and brutally kills her goose. This scaled-down, almost cartoonish version of rape satisfies the Cossacks enough for them to welcome them into their circle, but the narrator is haunted by his act of violence and its cost—that is, his sense of himself.

Savitsky is the Red Cavalry's Sixth Division Commander, and a physically large, imposing figure. While dashing off threats to murder other officers, should they fail at their mission, he is the first person the narrator encounters among the Cossacks. His blunt condescension toward the narrator—stemming from the narrator's glasses, stature, intellect, and sensibilities, all of which are presumably wrapped up in his stereotypical "Jewishness"— signal what pre-formed prejudices the narrator will confront while trying to work among the Cossacks.

The mistress is a bespectacled landlady, spinning yarn on the porch of her hut. She seems resigned to what is occurring around her, and although she repeatedly says that what's happening makes her want to kill herself, she never takes action. When the narrator orders her to prepare the dead goose, she simply does so, repeating her suicide mantra.

The quartermaster is the man who carries the narrator's suitcase to the hut. He provides the narrator with the key to social acceptance and respect among the Cossacks: while men of learning are looked upon with disdain, a man who rapes a "clean lady" is lionized. The quartermaster appears to sympathize with the narrator, until he suddenly rushes among a group of shaving Cossacks in a courtyard and announces Liutov's presence, mocking him as a man of learning, and reiterating that he is only there because they have no say or choice in the matter.

The young Cossack soldier lets the narrator know that he is not welcome by "mooning" him, and passing gas, after the quartermaster throws the narrator's suitcase in the street. After the narrator kills the goose and orders the landlady to cook it, however, the young soldier makes room for him in the Cossacks' circle and asks him about what is in the newspaper.

"My First Goose"

PATRICIA CARDEN ON SYMBOLISM

[Patricia Carden is the Director of Undergraduate
Studies at Cornell University, where she teaches courses
in Russian literature. Her book, *The Art of Isaac Babel*
was one of the first comprehensive works of Babel
scholarship in English, providing a thorough textual
analysis of most of his work; the book remains a
touchstone in the field.]

In "My First Goose" there is a double confrontation between
Cossack and narrator, narrator and the weak. The story opens
with a verbal duel between the narrator and that Cossack *par
excellence* Savitski in which attitudes on both sides are revealed.
Savitski challenges the narrator, "You're one of those pacifiers
and spectacles on your nose to boot. What a nasty little object."
But the narrator is helpless to defend himself, for he "envied the
flower and iron of that youth." The narrator's general
relationship with the Cossacks then is that they despise him and
he envies them and longs to be accepted by them. It is the
Cossacks who are in the position of judges and choosers. They
quickly make their choice and refuse to admit the narrator into
their circle. The narrator turns to the old woman in whose yard
they are camped to get food. The old woman immediately sees
that he is a kindred soul and appeals for sympathy: "'Comrade,'
she said after a pause, 'this business makes me want to hang
myself.'" Now the narrator is in the position of choice. Will he
acknowledge his kinship with the victimized, *bespectacled* old lady?
But what could be more damaging to his dream of acceptance by
the Cossacks than this instant recognition by the weak that he is
one of their own? "'Christ!' I muttered angrily and pushed the
old woman in the chest with my fist. 'I don't have to have
explanations with you.'" The goose is the symbolic offering to
the Cossacks that represents the narrator's willingness to accept

their way of things as well as the trigger to the brutal act against the old woman that signifies his rejection of her.

The narrator is caught between two standards: the Cossack standard of violence and assertion with justice as its chief moral principle, and the ethical standard of Babel's creative man with compassion and reconciliation as the chief moral principles. He recognizes in his own makeup a double weakness. He has the Cossack sense of outraged justice without the corresponding ability to act. Though passive he cannot accept humiliation or refrain from despising weakness. The narrator's double weakness casts a shadow of guilt across *Red Cavalry*.

—Patricia Carden, *The Art of Isaac Babel*. Ithaca: Cornell University Press, 1972: pp. 130–31.

MARTIN B. KLOTZ ON NARRATIVE VOICE

[Martin B. Klotz is now a partner in the New York law offices of Willkie, Farr & Gallagher, where he practices criminal law, securities law, and general litigation. He wrote this article, "Poetry of the Present: Isaac Babel's *Red Cavalry*," while pursuing his Ph.D. at Yale University.]

Living during the Russian revolution, Babel' was writing from within history rather than recalling a time safely past. Under the pressure of events memory could not do its healing work, leaving experience to disintegrate at times into a kaleidoscope of contradictions between what ought to be and what is, between past and present, Jew and Cossack, poet and commissar. As a narrative of ongoing events, then, *Red Cavalry* is a search for, rather than a revelation of, meaning. The narrator's tentative attitudes toward the events he is recounting are in a process of continual revision, and a stable perspective becomes a receding goal.

This persistent uncertainty can be felt in the opening scene of "My First Goose": "Savickij, Commander of the Sixth Division, rose when he saw me, and I was astonished at the beauty of his giant's body. He rose, and with the purple of his riding breeches, his cocked scarlet cap, the medals fixed on his breast, clove the hut in two, as a standard cleaves the sky. He smelled of perfume and the saccharine freshness of soap. His long legs resembled girls, bound to their shoulders in shining riding boots."[4] There is a Homeric majesty to the figure of Savickij; the repetition of the verb "rose" and the rhythm of Babel's description lend his movement an awesome grace. Savickij's beauty is static, he is an object set at a distance for contemplation, like a standard against the sky, while the image of his legs as girls bound in riding boots emphasizes that gender is transcended in an aesthetic object which is more than human. The narrator Ljutov surrenders to open and complete admiration of his Commander.

This initial impression is immediately undercut, however, by the hint of irony in the narrator's reference to the excess of scent about Savickij followed by the crudity that accompanies Savickij's recording of an order. He smears the entire sheet of paper with semiliterate prose that reveals his brutality: be threatens to execute his subordinate, not for failing to undertake, but for failing to succeed in his assigned mission. However, the narrator's irony is double-edged: his awareness of Savickij's brutality and vulgarity establishes not so much his superiority as his painful inability to accommodate himself to the Cossack ethos, within the context of which Savickij really is an epic hero. Belittlement of Savickij is the other side of the narrator's persistent isolation and unhappiness throughout *Red Cavalry*, and both are products of his overly subtle consciousness. His irony, directed against the confident heroism of the Cossacks, is thus uneasy and uncertain of its ground, and prone to turn on itself. Nonetheless it is effective irony, for it resists beguilement by the Cossack world. Victor Terras rightly observes that the conflict between Ljutov and the Cossacks is "a battle which both parties win and lose" (p. 145). The battle, however, is not a conflict between clearly defined principles with recognizable victories and defeats, but a never-ending battle in which principle and outcome are equally indefinite.

NOTE

4. I. Babel', *Konarmija, Odesskie Rasskazy, P'esy* (Letchworth, Herts.: Bradda, 1965), 49 (a reprint, except for "Moi listki—Odessa," from I. Babel', *Izbrannoe* [M.: GIXL, 1957]). All further page references are to this edition. Translations are my own, though throughout I have consulted Walter Morrison's excellent translation, Isaac Babel, *Collected Stories*, introd. Lionel Trilling (Cleveland: World, 1960).

   —Martin B. Klotz, "Poetry of the Present: Isaac Babel's Red Cavalry." *Slavic and East European Journal* 18, no. 2 (1974): pp. 160–61.

JOE ANDREW ON STRUCTURE

[Joe Andrew is a Lecturer in Russian Studies at the University of Keele in Great Britain, and he edited *The Structural Analysis of Russian Narrative Fiction*. His other works include *Russian Writers & Society in the Second Half of the Nineteenth Century*, *Women in Russian Literature: 1780–1863*, and *Writers & Society During the Rise of Russian Realism*. He is co-editor (with Robert Reid) of *Essays in Poetics* as well as co-chair of the Neo-Formalist Circle.]

'What matters is the introduction of a given motive at the moment when this motive achieves the greatest aesthetic effect'.[10] Also important, however, is the arrangement of the material to disclose the theme more clearly and fully to the reader. In the present instance a close examination of the narrative structure enables us to see that Babel was extremely careful to place the killing of the goose structurally (as well as thematically) at the very centre of the work, and thereby he seems to imply all the more strongly that we should look to this event for the meaning of the work.

The killing of the goose is formally marked off in a very clear fashion. Immediately before, and immediately afterwards, two phrases occur: 'I wish to hang myself' (the old woman) and 'Oh Mother of God!' (the narrator) (p. 55) which serve as a simple framing device to isolate the killing, off from the rest of the story. This mirror-image effect is highlighted by two references, immediately before and after the killing, to the woman's blindness, and perhaps even more significantly by the fact that the woman appears only immediately before the killing, and disappears immediately afterwards. The formal symmetry is not only satisfying aesthetically, but clearly serves a vital structural function: we are to treat the killing separately, as something set apart. Elsewhere, the narrative structure serves the function of comparing the narrator's situation before his central experience, and the new state of affairs. The parallels are striking and most successful in Babel's concentration on unity of effect. For example, at the beginning stress is laid on the fact that the author is literate: both Savitsky and the quartermaster point out the potential dangers of such a condition, yet it is precisely because he is an intellectual, and reads to the Cossacks, that he has his greatest success with them. (This is further deepened by the two references to Lenin's speech in *Pravda*. immediately before the killing the words mean nothing to him—afterwards he is exultant as he reads to them.) Originally, the Cossacks as a *group* (while shaving each other) reject him; later it is precisely in the group activity of a meal that they welcome him. This parallel, too, is underscored by the twin references to the Cossack with flaxen hair—it is he who emits the obscene noises which so crush the narrator and it is precisely he who asks for the reading. Clearly, *any* of them could have performed the second function, but Babel highlights the dramatic change by using the same character twice.

The change is indeed *dramatic*, involving as it does the crucial, central peripeteia. In general the story follows the traditional pattern of exposition—complication—crisis—dénouement, each of which takes place principally on the psychological level of the narrator's changing experience of the situation. The sequence is: exposition—narrator introduced to Cossack milieu, which is simultaneously sketched in; complication—he is rejected by them; crisis—his feelings of desolation, the killing of the goose; dénouement—acceptance by the Cossacks. As has been shown, the dénouement symmetrically matches the complication, which adds greatly to the power of the central episode. This power is also deepened by the absence of any general prologue or epilogue. As Oulanoff points out, this is typical of the short story, because it only has one 'knot' to be unravelled in order to end dramatically or unexpectedly.[11]

However, one must beware of oversimplification. The actual moment of peripeteia here may seem obvious enough (the killing of the goose), but perhaps the *real* turning point is a little earlier—that is when the narrator lays aside the newspaper and approaches the old woman.[12] It is then that he makes a decision even more crucial than to kill the goose. Indeed, one can point to several 'turning-points' in the story. When the narrator leaves Savitsky's office, he enters the wider world to meet his test; the threatened violence builds up, and then becomes actual violence (when the Cossacks throw him out), and immediately afterwards he is alone, for the first time. Then comes the psychological peripeteia—he lays aside the newspaper, and speaks and acts like the others had done—brutally and cruelly—which leads immediately to the actual killing. So, in one sense this event is only the culmination of a whole series of climaxes, each marked off by being a particular 'first-time' event. The extremely skilful use of the narrative structure by Babel not only serves to emphasise the reversal element, but marks off the series of climaxes leading to the central one.

NOTES

10. H. Oulanoff, *The Serapion Brothers, Theory and Practice*, (The Hague, 1966), p. 133.

11. Ibid., pp. 139–40.

12. I am indebted to Mr. Robin Milner-Gulland for first drawing my attention to this detail.

> —Joe Andrew, "Babel's 'My First Goose.'" *The Structural Analysis of Russian Narrative Fiction*. Staffordshire: Keele University, 1984: pp. 66–68.

PETER STINE ON IMAGERY

[Peter Stine is a faculty member at Oakland Community College in Michigan, where he is the chief editor of *Witness*, a literary journal. His articles have appeared in *Modern Fiction Studies*, *The Cambridge Quarterly*, *Contemporary Literature*, *Conradiana*, and *The South Atlantic Quarterly*, and he has edited the books *The Sixties* and *Sports in America*.]

This issue of violence is what checks Lyutov's desire, born of fancied inadequacies, to identify with the Cossacks. Joining the brigade in "My First Goose," he stands in voyeuristic awe of Savitsky, whose "long legs were like girls sheathed to the neck in shining riding boots" (*CS*, p. 73). But he is snubbed and hazed by the men as a "brainy type," told to "go out and mess up a lady ... and you'll have the boys patting you on the back" (*CS*, p. 74). What Lyutov does to earn their homoerotic company is seize the goose of an imploring peasant woman and brutally kill it with a sword. That night he reads the *Red Trooper* aloud around the campfire and "rejoiced, spying out exultingly the secret curve of Lenin's straight line" (*CS*, p. 76). But later: "I dreamed: and in my dreams saw women. But my heart, stained with bloodshed, grated and brimmed over" (*CS*, p. 77). These rites of initiation involve a violation of the soul. That childhood trauma of having his own pigeon smashed against his face during a pogrom is both normative and ineradicable. Hence when the issue is killing humans, Lyutov turns stillborn. Accused by the epileptic Akinfiev of taking an unloaded revolver into battle, he drives his antagonist away, but that evening "I continued on my way, imploring fate to grant me the simplest of proficiencies—the ability to kill my fellow-men" (*CS*, p. 187). This incapacity operates beyond psychology, is an ontological grounding, and under some circumstances is recognized as a moral weakness. When Lyutov comes upon the wounded Dolgushov, who asks to be mercifully dispatched to escape Polish torture, he leaves the chore for Alfonka, to whom he explains ("with a wry smile"): "I couldn't, you see" (*CS*, p. 90). This admits an element of squeamishness in Lyutov's abstension, as well as something else.

"Get out of my sight," his friend mutters, "or I'll kill you. You guys in specs have about as much pity for chaps like us as a cat has for a mouse" (*CS*, p. 90).

This charge is rebutted by the expansive pity shown for the plight of the Cossacks, but only to a degree. An element of exploitation remains. Good and evil interpenetrate in *Red Cavalry*, and Lyutov is no exception. Ultimately he must accept the charge of weakness leveled by those bloodied men "busy shelling and getting at the kernel for you" (*CS*, p. 129). *Red Cavalry* is utterly free of self-righteousness or hypocrisy on this matter. Any witness of stature knows he is as responsible for what he sees as for what he does. "What is our Cossack?" Babel wrote in his diary. "Layers of trashiness, daring, professionalism, revolutionary spirit, bestial cruelty."[22] These realities are now what this spy knows, for our sake. By delivering in silence his dazzling images of the Cossacks, Babel runs the risk of becoming a scapegoat for their deeds.[23]

NOTES

22. Quoted in Falen, p. 194.

23. We are in the habit of equating silence with complicity, but Babel's silence is the opposite, inviting us as readers to exercise what the Revolution had interdicted: individual moral judgment.

—Peter Stine, "Isaac Babel and Violence." *Modern Fiction Studies*, 30, no. 2 (1984): pp. 247–48.

EFRAIM SICHER ON ESTRANGEMENT AND IDENTITY

[Efraim Sicher teaches at Ben-Gurion University of the Negev. He is the author of a book and several essays about Isaak Babel, and has edited three volumes of Babel's prose. His publications also cover a wide range of topics in comparative literature from Dickens and George Eliot to Arnold Wesker and dystopian fiction.]

In Babel's short stories, the narrator is often a Jewish intellectual torn between his roots in the dying Jewish past and the Russian world of nature. This dilemma was typical of the young generation of Russian-speaking secular Jews in the early twentieth century who in the face of pogroms and discrimination turned to the growing Jewish national revival or to one of the revolutionary movements. The simultaneous attraction to the sensuous non-Jewish world and moral repulsion from its murderous amorality and anti-Semitism are expressed in a binary opposition of one's own (*rodnoi*): to alien (*chuzhoi*), associated with respectively open and closed spaces.[1] The narrator is pulled between, on the one hand, the open world of nature and sexuality and, on the other hand, the closed world of the Jewish past, ruined by pogroms, war, and revolution, from which he is forever breaking free but to which he is nostalgically drawn.

In the *Red Cavalry* story "My First Goose" the divisional commander Savitsky, whose powerful and sensuous body cuts across the hut, warns him that around here they cut the throats of guys with spectacles like him. The dying sun and the yellow pumpkin of the road are not reassuring. The illiterate Cossacks greet him by throwing out of the open courtyard where they have encamped his suitcase of manuscripts—the sign, along with his spectacles, of his alien identity.

Ironically, the narrator emphasizes how unacceptable he is as a Jew and an intellectual by showing his own degradation and admiring the face of the young peasant lad making obscene gestures at him. The narrator's hunger and loneliness intensify the sense of his otherness. The smoke from the Cossack's pot, in which they are cooking unkosher pork, is likened to smoke from one's own home ("*rodnoi dom*"). He gives up reading Lenin's speech in *Pravda* and takes the quartermaster's earlier advice to "mess up a lady." The violation is symbolic: he treads into dung the virgin white neck of a goose and sabers the landlady's sexual surrogate with "someone else's sword" ("*chuzhuiu sabliu*"). Only when he behaves like the Cossacks, killing, swearing, and hitting a woman's breasts, do they accept him into their ritual communion. They sit around their cooking pot like priests ("*zhretsy*") and invite him to eat with them while the landlady's goose is (literally) being cooked.

Only then does the Cossack who first insulted the narrator so vulgarly allow him to regain his role of bespectacled intellectual and read to them Lenin's speech at the second Comintern congress. They let him sleep with them, their legs intertwined and warming each others' bodies. However, acceptance has come at a price. As the last line tells us, at heart he cannot accept the Cossack ways. The killing of the goose is carried out in travesty of kosher slaughter and in desecration of the Jewish ethical code (as made explicit in a contemporary caricature by Boris Efimov).[2] The landlady whom he victimizes is half-blind and herself wears the spectacles which identify the educated intellectual and the victim; they both belong to the closed, non-Cossack indoor world. The Cossack world remains morally and topographically other *(chuzhoi)* and the intellectual narrator does not succeed in crossing to the other side of the transitional space of the courtyard. The story ends with the echo in the narrator's dreams of his crushing of the goose's neck: "Ia videl sny i zhenshchiny vo sne, i tol'ko serdtse moe, obagrennoe ubiistvom, skripelo i teklo." (I dreamed and there were women in my dreams, and only my heart, stained by murder, squealed and bled).[3] Despite the sexual and social communion of the Cossacks, the narrator cannot silence the moral Jewish voice within him.

For all the ambivalence of the authorial position, this dynamic opposition of imagery drives the dialectic throughout the *Red Cavalry* cycle. The values and characteristics of the Cossack *skaz* narrators are ideologically and ethnically hostile to those of closed areas with which they associate the intellectual in specs, the Jew who does not fight, the scribbling theoretician and administrator. By this logic Balmashev in "Salt" thinks of the Bolshevik leader Lenin as a Jewish communist and Trotsky, the commissar for war and a Jew, as the son of a Tambov governor who went over to the proletariat! This was, incidentally, a common confusion, as Trotsky commented on reading Babel's story.[4] In a later story, "Argamak," added to editions of *Red Cavalry* in 1933, the narrator does learn how to ride a horse with the Cossacks without drawing their enmity, but not before he has angered them for wanting to live without enemies.

NOTES

1. On binary opposition in Russian cultural modeling systems see Vjacheslav V. Ivanov and V.N. Toporov, *Slavianskie iazykovye modeliruiushchie sistemy: Drevnii period* (Moscow: Nauka, 1965), pp. 156-75; Iurii M. Lotman, *The Structure of the Artistic Text* (Ann Arbor: University of Michigan, 1977); Efraim Sicher, "Binary Oppositions and Spatial Representation: Towards an Applied Semiotics," *Semiotica* 60, 3-4 (1986): 211-224.

2. Reproduced in Isaak Babel, *Detstvo i drugie rasskazy*, ed. Efraim Sicher (Jerusalem: Biblioteka Aliya, 1979), p. 128.

3. *Detstvo i drugie rasskazy*, p. 132.

4. Leon Trotsky, *My Life* (Harmondsworth: Penguin Books, 1975), p. 376.

> —Efraim Sicher, "The Alien Voice." *Style and Structure in the Prose of Isaak Babel*. Columbus: Slavica, 1986: pp. 86. Revised especially for this volume.

YURI SHCHEGLOV ON THEMES AND ARCHETYPES

[Yuri Shcheglov is a Professor in the Department of Slavic Languages at the University of Wisconsin in Madison. He has co-written a number of books with fellow Babel scholar Alexander Zholkovsky, including *The Author's World and the Structure of the Text: Essays on Russian Literature* and *Poetics of Expressiveness: a Theory and Applications*.]

"My First Goose" is a paradigmatic text in more ways than one. Liutov's two encounters—first with the dazzling Savitskii and then with the ruthless and hostile warriors by the fire—illustrate the insoluble duality not only of the hero but of the new reality itself in which there are two inseparable and constantly overlapping facets that can roughly he called "romantic" and "barbaric." This is a dilemma confronted by many heroes of early Soviet fiction who are spontaneously drawn to the revolution yet are dismayed by the discrepancy between the realm of its enthusiastic theorists, poets and visionaries; and that of barbarians, fanatics, dullards or bureaucrats who violently and thoughtlessly translate exciting ideals into disappointing realities. This theme has a wide spectrum of variations in the Soviet fiction dealing with the revolution and its aftermath, socialism; apart from "My First Goose," we recognize it in Olesha's *Envy* in which Kavalerov may secretly desire to join the charismatic Andrei Babichev but is repelled by the narrow-minded brutality of his disciple, Volodia Makarov. This duality of the revolution is famously presented in Sholokhov's *Quiet Flows the Don*, as well as in Pasternak's *Doctor Zhivago*, in the novels of Il'f and Petrov[13] and in other major works of Soviet fiction. (...)

Reading the story in a sound realistic key (that is, temporarily leaving aside its rich literary and archetypal subtext), one cannot fail to notice that the narrator deliberately treats his hosts to a rather coarse, slapstick show. The theatricality of his performance is manifest from the sheer redundancy of the sword that Liutov picks up from the ground to no apparent use, as well as from the exaggerated belligerence of his gesticulation and speech, rather comic in a little, bespectacled civilian addressing an old woman, yet accepted at face value by his viewers.[14] Liutov's mimicry and calculated simulation as a means of recognition distinguishes him rather sharply from the majority of the intelligentsia heroes of early Soviet fiction, both those who are locked in a love–hate relationship with the revolution and those who just hate it but feign loyalty for survival. Suffice it to compare Liutov with Olesha's Kavalerov, whose behavior in a similar context, whether demanding admission to the Soviet aviation parade or showering venomous philippics upon his nemesis, Andrei Babichev, is always passionate and straightforward. Liutov's vacillation between his readiness to exploit the simplicity of the Red Cavalry heroes, to gain their favors by cunning, on the one hand, and his secret envy for the "flower and iron of their youth," on the other, is a more complex stance. It reminds us not so much of the dismayed intellectuals of a Kavalerov type as of wise, thoroughly experienced Ostap Bender of the last part of *The Golden Calf*, who, when confronted with the army of enthusiastic builders of the great Turkish railway, is not sure which he desires more, to continue playing his picaresque tricks and manipulating their still rather simple souls for his personal gain, or to lay down his arms and tearfully beg for admission into their happy community.

Another curious detail in the surface plot of "My First Goose" is the role played by Lenin's name and text as a form of lingua franca which functions as the final mediator between Liutov and the Cossacks after they have been sufficiently "mollified" by his cavalier treatment of the landlady. In early Soviet mythology the name "Lenin" tends to figure as a password that overcomes distances and class/race barriers (e.g. in Vsevolod Ivanov's *Armored*

Train 14–69 where the partisans intone the word "Lenin" to get their message across to their American prisoner; in Nikolai Tikhonov's poem, "Sami," etc.). As many other details of the story, this one has an obvious realistic motivation, since Lenin's persona embraced the contrasting halves of the revolution, both theory and practice, and appealed to individuals otherwise divided, educated fellow travelers and brutal bolshevik warriors.[15] At the same time, serving as a kind of magic "sesame," the name preserves a subdued aura of mystique that agrees well with the mythologizing, ritualistic and fairy-tale-like connotations of the story.

Although more could be said about the plot, symbolism and other aspects of "My First Goose," I shall now focus on my main topic, its *archetypal* patterns, that is, literary motifs of ancient, ritualistic and mythological origin which serve as a kind of concealed amplifier enhancing the paradigmatic effect of the story's events. The narrator's ambivalent attitude to the Red Cavalry warriors obviously influenced the selection of these archetypes, which fall into two categories. For that part of the narrator's soul which craves to be tested and accepted into the Cossack brotherhood, the appropriate archetypal counterpart is *Initiation* with its various ritualistic concomitants. The word "initiation" has been used previously in Babel' criticism (by Trilling, Andrew and others), but in a more figurative than terminological sense, that is, without sufficient awareness of those features in *Red Cavalry* which actually reflect the traditional ordeals that adolescents had to undergo to become full-fledged members of their society.

For the other half of his hero's persona, which responds to the revolution with a mixture of intellectual curiosity, estrangement, fear, revulsion and mimicry, Babel' drew not so much on ritualistic sources as on legendary and literary ones; more specifically, on motifs that have to do with *Visiting the Otherworld*. This is a well known topos whose protagonist is an individualist, an outsider who undertakes a journey to forbidden regions to obtain something for himself—an object, a human being, a benefit, a piece of arcane wisdom, etc. To achieve his objective, the hero may have to play the games of the inhabitants of the otherworld, to spy out their secrets, to use stratagems, to cheat and to flee for his life.

Since the initiation rites also imply a journey to the country of the dead, some degree of overlap between the two sets of archetypal motifs is to be expected. However, each of the two groups includes some motifs that are distinctly its own, i.e., either initiatory or demonic par excellence. More importantly, even identical motifs may acquire different overtones depending on which set is activated: with *Initiation* the stress is likely to be on the hero's desire to be assimilated, to submit to ordeals, to fraternize with his new companions and to obey his seniors; while *Visiting the Otherworld* will highlight the dangers and risks of the enterprise, that realm's basic viciousness and hostility to man, and the hero's independence.

NOTES

13. The relationship between the ideal and real, "earthly" socialism in Il'f and Petrov is discussed in Iu. K. Shcheglov, *Romany I. Il'fa i E. Petrova* (Wien: *Wiener Slawistischer Almanach*, Sonderband 26/1 and 26/2, 1990–91), 11–24.

14. In a similar manner the hero of Babel's "My First Honorarium" (1928) wins a prostitute's personal sympathy and successfully passes his sexual initiation by making her believe a fictional story of his life (note the parallelism of titles).

15. Ironically, it is the same duality of Lenin that enables Liutov to maintain his inner distance: far from merging with his audience in a cathartic co-experience, he leaves it to the Cossacks to enjoy the sheer force and directness of Lenin's speech ("he goes and strikes at it straight off like a hen pecking at a grain") while secretly relishing Lenin's more recondite dialectics ("I read on and rejoiced, spying out exultingly the secret curve of Lenin's straight line"). The issue of "straight line" vs. "curve" in connection with Liutov's duality and with the compromise between him and the Cossacks is convincingly discussed by Andrew ("Structure and Style in the Short Story," 19).

—Yuri Shcheglov, "Some Themes and Archetypes in Babel's Red Cavalry." *Slavic Review* 53, no. 3 (Fall 1994): 657–59.

"The Story of My Dovecote"

"The Story of My Dovecote," like "My First Goose," has a
deceptively cheerful title, one that suggests a tale about a child's
interactions with his birds. While the innocence that the title
suggests is present, and is in fact an important component in the
story, it is harshly, violently undercut by the story's end.

The narrator explains at the outset that as a child, he wanted
a dovecote badly, thus establishing that the narrator is now
temporally far-removed from his childhood. In 1904, he says, he
was nine years old, living in Nikolayev, and preparing for
examinations. The narrator was frightened of the exams,
knowing that the Jewish entry quota for the Nikolayev Lycée
(high school) was five percent; specifically, out of forty boys, only
two Jews would make the cut. His father promised to buy the boy
doves if he scored the highest possible on two of the exams, and
this tormented the child, who, out of anxiety, slipped into a
dream-state while taking the exam. Critics have often noted that
the narrator's dream-state indicates that he is a Babelian man-in-
training, because adult men in Babel's work—particularly Jewish
fathers, as is true with this story—live in their dreams and their
imagination, constantly thinking about how their families, or
specifically their children, might bring success, fame, and/or
prestige to the family. In this way, the boy's daydreams during the
exam are not only an escape from the pressure to succeed, but
also an initial step toward becoming like his father. In spite of his
mental wanderings, the boy's exam scores were among the
highest.

Due to circumstances beyond the boy's control, however, the
high test scores were not enough. Khariton Efrussi, a rich, Jewish
grain merchant and exporter, managed to arrange a Lycée
appointment for own his son by way of a bribe, and the narrator's
score was thus lowered by one to accommodate Efrussi Junior.
The narrator's father, heartbroken, wanted to attack Efrussi, or
hire two dockworkers to do the job—thus turning to violence
when his dreams were thwarted—but his wife talked him out of

it. Here, we see the typical Babelian mother figure, so much a realist as to be pessimistic. A perfect counter to the father, the mother figures in Babel's stories think that nothing will get better; or if a situation improves, it's only temporary; these women perpetually wait for the other shoe to drop, knowing, to a certainty, that it will.

The narrator continues with his story, telling us he studied even harder for the next year's examination. The family secretly arranged for the narrator's tutor to teach him the material from the Lycée preparatory course as well as the first year, so the narrator learned three books by heart: a grammar book, a math book, and a Russian history text.

The narrator's schoolmaster, Karavayev, barely thirty, with a peasant's complexion and a hairy wart on his face, presided over the second examination, along with the deputy warden, who asked the boy about Peter I. The narrator first went blank and panicked, but then he remembered the passages about Peter the Great in the Russian history book, as well as in Pushkin's poems. While crying and shivering, the boy shouted the verses of the poems rapidly, continuing a long time until the deputy warden, Pyatnitsky, leaned toward Karavayev and said, "What a nation! The devil is in these Yids!" Thus, even when "praising" the narrator, Pyatnitsky tosses off an inherently anti-Semitic statement, demonstrating that above and beyond harsh admission quotas, Jews could never transcend the deeply embedded prejudice that surrounded them—even in those who would appear to champion them, as Pyatnitsky did the narrator.

Pyatnitsky dismissed the boy, who went into the hallway and snapped out of his trance. Pyatnitsky soon appeared in the corridor and told the other children to leave the narrator alone, then told the narrator that he would be in the first class.

The boy went to his father's store to tell him the news. With undying optimism, the father closed the shop and took him out to buy a cap with the school emblem. The response of the boy's mother, however, was mixed; she embraced the boy one minute, pushed him away the next; clearly, she was preparing herself (as previously noted) for the disaster that would surely follow this good news. She argued that a list would appear in the newspaper of those students admitted—and God would punish them, and people would laugh, if the family bought the uniform prematurely—and then she stared at her son with pity, already mourning for his pre-ordained heartbreak.

The narrator next explains that the men in his family were traditionally too trusting and impulsive, and provides examples. The narrator's father continually offended people with his openness, so they cheated him, though the father interpreted his bad luck as malevolent fate. The narrator was the mother's only hope, though he states, "Like all Jews, I was short in stature, weak, and plagued by headaches from too much study." Here, the narrator's self-loathing in regard to his Jewishness becomes apparent. Readers can see, by way of his development throughout the story, that the boy not only learned how others viewed him because of his Jewish background, but also to view himself through this same external lens, which wreaks havoc on his evolving sense of self.

The names of the next class were posted outside the Lycée, and the narrator's whole family went to look, including Grandpa Shoyl, the boy's great uncle and a braggart who sold fish in the market. Shoyl told fabricated stories about the Polish uprising of 1861, tall tales that always entertained his nephew and others.

The narrator's father arranged for a celebratory feast, inviting grain merchants, estate brokers, and agricultural salesmen. The narrator noted that the salesmen were generally the most worldly and cheerful, and that Old Liberman, who taught the child Hebrew and the Torah, made a toast, declaring that the boy had won a victory over the rich and privileged. He compared the event to David felling Goliath, and said the Jews would triumph over their oppressors and enemies through "sheer power of mind." He wept as he finished, then everyone danced, and the narrator's mother even took a sip of wine. She didn't like vodka and didn't understand how anyone could, just as she couldn't understand how any women lived with Russian husbands. This is the mother's response to the widespread anti-Semitism in Russia: she rejects the lifestyle, objects, and customs of those who, to her, are the "other," in the same oversimplified, unquestioning manner that they reject hers.

Happiness, for the narrator's mother, began when she made him sandwiches in the morning, and went shopping with him for school supplies. They both reveled in the newness of the items, and only after a month of this contentment did the boy remember the doves. He received a dovecote from Grandpa Shoyl, made from a box and painted brown, and he had the money for the doves, so he planned a Saturday trip to the wild game market.

At this point, the narrator retreats from the story to provide historical context, stating that in the fall of 1905, Czar Nicholas was giving the people a constitution, and speechmakers were orating on the street, outside town council buildings. Gunshots were heard at night, and the narrator's mother grew wary about his trip to the wild game market. On the Saturday morning he planned to go, kids went by on the street, flying a kite, and the baker's sons pulled a vaulting horse outside, while an out-of-uniform constable encouraged their stunts. Bizarrely, this official in casual clothes was what worried the mother, who forbade the boy's market venture. However, the boy sneaked out the back yard and ran to the square.

Ivan Nikodimich, the dove seller, occupied his usual space, and the narrator purchased two pairs, hiding them in a sack beneath his shirt. The boy had money still, but the man wouldn't sell a male and female Kryukov dove at that price. As the market closed, however, and Nikodimich saw no other buyers, he called the boy back over. The narrator notes: "Things turned out my way, things turned out badly." In this small moment, the narrator demonstrates a sensibility inherited from his mother, who always expected the worst to happen to herself and her family. At first glance this would appear to contradict the idea that the boy had been in a Babelian male-in-training at the time of the exams; but because the story is narrated from an adult's perspective, readers should note this single sentence acts as a clue, indicating that an event will soon disrupt this training (and indeed, the story's forthcoming climax catalyzes the narrator's transition from optimist to realist in relatively short order).

A man in boots walked across the square then, telling the dove seller "in town the nobles of Jerusalem are being given a constitution. On Rybnaya Street they've just served Grandpa Babel a helping of death." (Interestingly, there is no response from the narrator at the news of his great uncle's murder, perhaps establishing the dreamy remove and distance of which the boy is still capable at this moment.) The dove seller muttered, then shouted, that this was wrong while he gathered his animals and pushed the Kryukov doves into the boy's hands. The boy hid them under his shirt, too, then watched people flee from the market, which quickly emptied.

He heard shots and ran, dashing into an alley where he found Makarenko, a normally friendly, legless, wheelchair-bound man who sold cigarettes around town. The boy ran to him and asked if he had seen his great uncle Shoyl. The man didn't answer, fidgeting, while his wife, Katyusha, looked through objects scattered on the ground. Makarenko, ignoring the boy, asked her for an inventory report from their looting, and she told him that they had seven pairs of spats, six duvet covers, and several bonnets. Makarenko grew angry at the news and said that other people got fine things, and almost as proof of his words, a woman rushed through the alley with fezzes and a bolt of calico, calling out to her children. Makarenko tried to follow her and called out to her, but she vanished from sight, and a peasant in a cart going by asked where everyone had gone. Makarenko said everyone was going to Sobornaya Street, and begged him to bring any merchandise he could grab, since he would buy everything. The peasant rushed off in his cart, leaving Makarenko staring at the boy, asking him, "Well, am I not the man that God singled out?" He stretched out his leprous hand and snatched the boy's bag from him, then pulled out a cherry-red dove. He approached the boy and slapped him across the face, crushing the bird in the process. (Notably, a bird dies a violent death here, just as one does in "My First Goose," a recurring motif in Babel's work; however, the crime in this story seems particularly heinous, since doves are specifically associated with peace.) The boy fell, "in his new overcoat," and the wife rose and said, "Their seed has to be stamped out! ... I cannot abide their seed and their stinking men!"

Again, the masculinity of male Jews is called into question—

the boy isn't even a match for a leprosy-riddled, legless man—and Makarenko and the boy enact a small-scale pogrom of their own just as a large-scale one occurs around them. Through Makarenko, Babel shows Russians' sense of frustration and fury at their own seemingly helpless destitution, as well as their illogical but staunch placement of blame for their problems on Jews. For this reason, even though the boy has done nothing malevolent toward Makarenko, he receives harsh punishment—seemingly for wearing a new coat (a key detail) when the cripple and his wife are scrounging and looting for survival.

Having been knocked down, the boy lay with the bird's innards trickling down his face, blinding him; through his clear eye, the world looked "small and ugly" to him, and he focused on those items on the ground around him. In this moment, quite literally, the boy began to see the world around him from a new perspective. He closed his eyes, then walked through the streets and cried, "more fully and happily than I would ever cry again," which seems ironic, until readers consider what was lost and gained. Makarenko's violent blow acted as the starting point of a transition for the narrator, who lost his blissful ignorance about the world, as well as the dream-oriented perspective that painfully, heartbreakingly still consumed his father. (This childhood epiphany has caused some critics to draw a comparison between James Joyce's story "Araby" in *Dubliners* and "The Story of My Dovecote.")

The boy, while walking, spotted a muzhik, or peasant farmer, who smashed Khariton Efrussi's window frame with a hammer and yelled. (In this way, Efrussi appears to receive punishment for his previous infraction against the narrator's family, though there is no relation between the two events.) A religious procession appeared, marching from the town council; old men carried a portrait of the Czar, and women ran in front. The muzhik stopped hammering and ran to join the procession, while the boy hid, waiting for it to go by so he could go home. Once he arrived, he found the house empty, with its doors open, and the grass around it trampled. Only Kuzma, the janitor, remained, sitting in the shed with Shoyl's dead body.

Kuzma told the boy that the townsfolk had "hacked" Shoyl

down, and pulled a perch from Shoyl's fishing rod. One perch had been shoved into Shoyl's mouth, too, and though he was dead, one of the fish was alive and quivering. Kuzma told the boy that only Shoyl had been killed, after cursing the Russians' "goddamn mothers up and down." He told the narrator that he should put two fivers on his eyes, but the boy didn't understand why. He whispered for Kuzma to save them, then embraced the man's back. Kuzma, meanwhile, busied himself with Shoyl's legs, then bound the man's jaws and combed his beard. He told the boy again that Shoyl cursed the Russians' mothers, and that "those damn Russians think it's an insult to forgive someone, I know those Russians well!" He poured sawdust on Shoyl, took off his apron, and grabbed the boy's hand, telling him that they should find the boy's father. The story ends, then, with the line, "And I went with Kuzma to the house of the tax inspector, where my parents had hidden from the pogrom."

Significantly, the word "pogrom" appears nowhere in the story until the very end, as the last word, thus providing it with great emotional weight and drama. The story's non-linear structure reflects the way Babel places his characters in the context of history. Unlike other Russian writers, for whom characters are, primarily, a convenient vehicle for examining history, Babel uses historical events to show us more about his characters, and how their sense of themselves is affected by the violence that surrounds them.

"The Story of My Dovecote"

The narrator is a boy who works out a deal with his father: if he gets accepted to the Nikolayer Lycée as one of the only two Jewish students allowed each year, his father will buy him doves, which he wants terribly. The boy scores second highest on the exam when he takes it the first time, but the son of a rich Jewish grain merchant, through bribes, takes the place of the narrator, whose grade is lowered. The next year, the boy scores the highest, and the day he sneaks out to buy his doves, a pogrom occurs. After buying the doves, he hides in an alley, where he finds a Russian cripple who sells cigarettes, Makarenko, and his wife, studying what they have managed to steal through looting. Makarenko takes the boy's package from him and becomes infuriated when he finds doves inside. He takes a bird and smashes it against the boy's face, and later, when the boy heads home, he finds that his boastful, storytelling uncle had been killed.

The narrator's father is the typical Babelian male: perpetually swept away by dreams of grandeur, he dismisses realistic limitations, and when his dreams are thwarted, he responds with anger and violence. Critics have pointed out that the father trains the boy to be the same sort of man, hinted at by the dream-like state the boy goes into while taking the exam both times, a result of the pressure the boy feels from the father to succeed. When a rich Jewish merchant buys the Lycée spot that the narrator rightfully earned, the boy's father wants to go beat him up, or hire men from the docks to do so.

The narrator's mother is the typical Babelian female: grounded in reality, to the point of relentless pessimism, she is constantly aware of the worst that can happen, so that when it does, she is unruffled. (Conversely, when it doesn't, she tiptoes through life, sure that it won't last.) When the narrator receives the news that he's accepted into the Lycée, for example, she worries about the father rushing out and buying the boy the school's hat, thinking that they will look foolish when the acceptance falls through; and later, when she sees a constable walking the street out of uniform, she forbids the boy from going to the market to buy doves, as he had planned, because she's panicked by such casual displays of freedom.

Pyatnitsky is the deputy warden, who is one of the two officiants giving the exam. He is impressed by the narrator's performance, but as many critics have pointed out, even his compliments have the ring of anti-Semitism.

Grandpa Shoyl is the narrator's uncle, and a beloved old braggart, who works at the fish market and tells tall tales, particularly about the Polish uprising of 1861. He is killed during the pogrom, left with a fish pushed into his mouth and another fish shoved into the fly of his pants.

Ivan Nikodimich is the vendor at the wild game market who sells the doves to the narrator. While finishing the transaction, Nikodimich hears from a passerby that Grandpa Shoyl has just been killed as an example to the Jewish community.

Makerenko is the destitute disabled Russian who sells cigarettes in the streets. The narrator finds him and his wife in an alley, where the boy runs when the market hurriedly clears out. The couple look through what they've gathered from looting, and Makerenko is bitter and dissatisfied with their plunder. He takes the paper bag from the narrator, removes one of the boy's doves, and slaps his face with it, so hard that the bird is crushed.

Katyusha, Makerenko's wife, while sorting through squalid looting treasures in an alley, voices anti-Semitic rhetoric in front of the narrator, saying that they must "stamp out" Jewish seed, and that she hates their "stinking men."

Khariton Efrussi is the rich Jewish grain merchant who, through bribes, manages to arrange for his own son to take the narrator's place at the Lycée. Near the end of the story, during the pogrom, a muzhik is seen smashing the windowpane of Efrussi's home.

Kuzma is the narrator's family's janitor, and the only person at the narrator's home when the boy returns. In the shed, Kuzma prepares Grandpa Shoyl for burial. He pulls the fish from Shoyl's mouth and his fly, and then tells the boy that Shoyl cursed the Russians to the very end. In the end, Kuzma takes the boy to the tax collector's, where his family had been hiding during the pogrom.

"The Story of My Dovecote"

Patricia Carden on Education

[Patricia Carden is the Director of Undergraduate Studies at Cornell University, where she teaches Russian literature. Her book, *The Art of Isaac Babel,* was one of the first comprehensive works of Babel scholarship in English, providing a thorough textual analysis of most of his work; the book remains a touchstone in the field.]

Babel shows the pressure of history and social circumstance upon the individual life. (...)

The story expands not only in the direction of the historical and social context but in the direction of the context of the family and the Jewish community. These tensions are encompassed in the boy's relationship with his father, centered in the father's generous promise to buy the longed-for doves, a promise hedged by his demands for outstanding performance in the admission examinations. This personal situation in the family extends to the situation in the Jewish community, for the child's admission to the school is a way of acquiring status for the family. When the grain dealer Khariton Efrussi buys his son's way into the gymnasium ahead of young Babel, who had earned the place, it is an indication of the father's failure, for had he succeeded in life he would have bought his son in. (...)

In the dreamlike atmosphere of the examination the child experiences his first moment of true knowledge and release:

> I knew about Peter the Great by heart from Putsykovich's history and from Pushkin's poems. I poured out these poems, the faces suddenly whirled around in my sight and became mixed up like cards from

a new pack. They reshuffled themselves on the retina of my eyes, and in these moments, trembling, drawing myself up, hurrying, I shouted Pushkin's verses with all my might. I shouted them at length. No one interrupted my insane mouthings. Through a crimson blindness, through the freedom that overcame me, I saw only the old, inclined face of Piatnitski with his silver-streaked beard.

The freedom the child experiences is the freedom of dream. He gives himself up totally to the imaginary world of his learning, and for the moment even the reality of the examination with its pressures slips away from him. The escape from reality into the world of the imagination is one of the poles of freedom. The first movement of the story, the "school" movement, reaches its climax here. The pattern is one of tension and release.

But before the movement ends, there are two preparatory developments of theme. The coercion by the father, the stress of the examinations, the freedom of performance have all been for the child flights from knowledge of his situation. He has lived in a special world. Now we are again reminded of the child's ambiguous relationship to the external world. As he waits outside the examining room for word of success or failure, he is stalked as prey by the Russian schoolboys. Sensing danger, he "wakes up" from his fatigue-induced reverie. He is saved by the kindly intervention of Piatnitski; thus his knowledge of the realities of the world in which he must live remains incomplete. (...)

The Babel menfolk are an interesting breed, rebels, dreamers, madmen. They all have only a tenuous hold on reality, but their incipient madness leads them into lives of adventure like Uncle Lev (who kidnaped the daughter of a supply officer and fled with her to California, where he abandoned her and "died in a house of ill repute among Negroes and Malays") or into poetry like the inspired liar Shoyl.

Now the child is being educated into the Babel madness, and the symptoms of delirium are upon him. This leads to conflict with the mother, who takes a different view of the world. (...)

The mother's clear-sighted view of the realities of their situation leads her to withdraw before the hostile world. She fears to buy a school cap too soon, for "God would punish us and people would laugh at us." (...)

In the first half of the story, Babel sets in opposition Jew and Russian, desire and coercion; the historical and the private, knowledge from books and knowledge of life, dreams and illusion. The characters are defined by the ways in which they fit into or react to these categories. But the process of definition of the categories becomes increasingly complicated as they cross into one another and blur. The Jew Efrussi is more the enemy of the Babel father and son than the Russian teacher Karavaev, who wishes the boy well. Karavaev's physical characteristics are emphasized, and it is a clear portrait of the enemy. His blond ruddiness links him with the peasant looters of the latter half of the story. Yet he is capable of feeling joy "for me and for Pushkin" when the child declaims Pushkin's verses on Peter the Great. There are categories in the story that transcend race, and the first of these is art and the community of art. Thus we see a pressure at work in the story toward a proper alignment of values, a pressure to find the true categories that "work" by supplying reliable information about the world.

—Patricia Carden, *The Art of Isaac Babel.* Ithaca: Cornell University Press, 1972: pp. 155, 156–58, 158–59, 160.

PETER STINE ON VIOLENCE

[Peter Stine is a faculty member at Oakland Community College in Michigan, where he is the chief editor of *Witness*, a literary journal. His articles have appeared in *Modern Fiction Studies*, *The Cambridge Quarterly*, *Contemporary Literature*, *Conradiana*, and *The South Atlantic Quarterly*, and he has edited the books *The Sixties* and *Sports in America*.]

Judging from his stories of his childhood, we may conclude that Babel knew death as illumination from an early age. It came with an outbreak of anti-Semitism, that "black vileness" that he admitted to Paustovsky was the one thing he could never comprehend.[3] Indeed his indelible images of violence seem to suggest a state of lucid, mesmerized incredulity. In "The Story of My Dovecot" the short, weakly, ten-year-old prodigy passes his exams into the secondary school of Nikolayev, only to be victimized by a czarist-sponsored pogrom the day he goes to claim his reward. His elders herald his feat as a victory over "the foes who had encircled us and were thirsting for our blood,"[4] but this Jewish faith in learning is exploded when the boy is assaulted with his beloved pigeons by a legless cigarette vendor in the murderous streets:

> I lay on the ground, and the guts of the crushed bird trickled down from my temple. They flowed down my cheek, winding this way and that, splashing, blinding me. The tender pigeon-guts slid down over my forehead, and I closed my solitary unstopped eye so as not to see the world that spread out before me. This world was tiny, and it was awful. A stone lay just before my eyes, a little stone so chipped as to resemble the face of an old woman with a large jaw. A piece of string lay not far away, and a bunch of feathers that still breathed. My world was tiny, and it was awful. I closed my eyes so as not to see it, and pressed myself tight into the ground that lay beneath me in soothing dumbness. This trampled earth in no way resembled real life, waiting for exams in real life. Somewhere far away Woe rode across it on a great steed, but the noise of the hoofbeats grew weaker and died away, and silence, the bitter silence that sometimes overwhelms children in their sorrow, suddenly deleted the boundary between body and the earth that was moving now hither. The earth smelled of raw depths, of the tomb, of flowers. I smelled its smell and started crying, unafraid. I was

walking along an unknown street set on either side with
white boxes, walking in a getup of bloodstained feathers,
alone between the pavements swept clean as on Sunday,
weeping bitterly, fully and happily as I never wept again
in my life. (*CS*, pp. 262–263)

Here violence tears a veil from reality, compelling wonder, as the
boy dies from innocence, even selfhood, into a zone of
perceptual joy beyond fear or shame. Such is the mental state of
one upon returning, as it were, from the dead—and this would be
the ground of the *joie de vivre* and sunlit aesthetics of this deeply
eschatological writer. Yet if the world for the survivor is renewed
in a cosmic embrace, he also has special obligations. Returning
home, the boy comes upon his grandfather murdered, fish stuck
in his mouth and trousers, one "still alive, and struggling" (*CS*, p.
264). This symbol of degradation would later take voice in the
undercurrents of Babel's art: a subterranean link with the victims
of violence affixed forever.

Notes

3. "I didn't choose to be born a Jew," Babel told Paustovsky. "I think I can
understand everything. Only not the reason for that black vileness they call anti-
semitism. I came safely through a Jewish pogrom as a child, only they tore my
pigeon's head off. Why?" *Yeast of Hope*, p. 141.

4. Isaac Babel, *The Collected Stories*, trans, and ed. by Walter Morison (New
York: Criterian Books, 1955). p. 257. Further references, abbreviated *CS*, will be
included parenthetically within the text.

> —Peter Stine, "Isaac Babel and Violence." *Modern Fiction Studies*
> 30, no. 2 (1984): pp. 247–48.

Hamutal Bar-Yosef on Stereotypes and Storytelling

[Hamutal Bar-Yosef is a poet and researcher of modern
Hebrew literature and philosophy, concentrating on
Jewish-Russian writers. Her publications include *On
Zelda's Poetry*, *Decadent Trends in Modern Hebrew
Literature*, and *Symbolism in Modern Poetry*.]

Jewishness has many faces in "The Story of My Dovecot" as well. There are the Jewish nouveaux riches, merchants of unbounded ambition, such as Khariton Efrussi who bribes an official to get his son into the Russian secondary school. There is the Jewishness of naive people, dreamers of dreams, acting without thinking. "All the men in our family were trusting by nature, and quick to ill-considered actions" (p. 223).[4] There is the pathetically aggressive, ridiculous Zionism of Lieberman, the Hebrew teacher. There is the Jewishness of the mother, the only clear-sighted person in the story and therefore a pessimist, and there is, of course, the Jewishness of the child-narrator, who distinguishes himself in passing the test of cultural acceptability, but immediately undergoes the shock of blind xenophobia. The Gentiles in the story are equally many-sided. There is the sick sadism of Makarenko and the psychopathic racism of his wife, but there is also the antisemitic examiner who is open to conviction, and the bird-seller—a figure of folk magic—who says "They shouldn't!" (p. 228) of the pogrom. There is also the janitor Kuzma, a fine father figure.

However, with all Babel's hesitation and ambivalence as regards the subject of Jewishness, it can safely be said that "The Story of My Dovecot" (with its sequel "First Love") represents a significant turning point in his attitude to his Jewish identity. The *Red Cavalry* cycle reflects the change in Babel's attitude to Jewishness as a result of his encounter with Polish Jews during his movements with the Red Army during the post-revolutionary civil war. The change is expressed chiefly in his readiness to regard the Jewish condition as one of suffering and victimization. In "The Rabbi's Son," the final story in *Red Cavalry* (1924 version), the narrator accepts his personal part in this destiny, recognizing his inability to run away from it. "The Story of My Dovecot" (1925) goes further in this direction, and represents the narrator's autobiographical memories as a distinctively Jewish autobiography. (...)

The plot of "The Story of My Dovecot" consists of two fabulae, each centering upon a traumatic experience: the entrance examination and the pogrom. The connecting link between them is the dovecot promised to the child as a reward (or a bribe) if he passes the examination, but brutally torn from him by the pogrom. The title, read literally (in Russian: "Istoria moyei golubyatni," "istoria" meaning both "a story" and "a history," see below), prepares the reader for some kind of animal stories about a child and a beloved pet, such as "The Calf" by Feierberg. The familiar connotations of the dove as a symbol of love and tenderness (in Russian, as well as in Hebrew and Yiddish) contribute to the false anticipation aroused by the title.

At the first reading the Secondary School entrance examination appears to be the central event of the story, both thematically and emotionally. This impression, if proved correct, would assign "The Story of My Dovecot," together with "Childhood. At Grandmother's" and "The Awakening," to a group of stories whose main subject is family pressure on the gifted child, forcing him into extraordinary scholarly achievements. This pressure stems from illusory expectations for the future: "My Granny believed me, believed in me and wanted me to become a great lord when I grow up. ("Childhood. At Grandmother's," p. 31). In "The Awakening" the father attempts to turn his son into a famous violin virtuoso.

In these two stories the compulsive pressure is characteristic of only certain members of the family (the father and the grandmother, but not the mother); however, it is also presented as a pathological trait of Jews of a certain social standing in assimilated Jewish society, who want their children to achieve the high, even noble, social position they themselves lack: "All the folk in our circle—brokers, shopkeepers, clerks in banks and steamship offices—used to have their children taught music" ("The Awakening," p. 267); "... but though my father could have reconciled himself to poverty, fame he must have" (ibid., p. 268). The author represents this Jewish ambition as self-deception based on empty family pride: "'It's not possible,' people feeding at his expense would insinuate, that the grandson of such a grandfather ..." (ibid.). He sees in it both a cultural anachronism and a threat to the sensual vitality of the child, degenerating into sterility and cruelty. This form of the theme recalls motifs from the Hebrew Haskalah literature which accused Jewish religious culture of evading the demands of "life." Here the same criticism is directed at semi-assimilated Jewish society remaining unchanged in this respect.

The theme appears again in the first part of "The Story of My Dovecot." The father's unlimited aspirations and dubious pedigree are criticized by implication, together with the whole cruel competitiveness forced upon Jews who wanted to send their children to Russian Secondary schools, which, before the revolution, practiced the numerus clausus system. The child fails his first examination because a rich Jewish merchant bribes the examiner: "My mark was changed from a to a minus, and Efraim Junior went to the secondary school instead of me" (p. 221). Still, Babel provides historical perspective in his exposition, taking the trouble to explain to the contemporary reader the problems imposed on Russian Jewry by the school regulations. At the same time he caricatures the Hebrew teacher's hope of national revival, and ridicules the exaggerated hysterical excitement, characteristic of both the teacher and the father, examples of emasculated Jewish manhood (p. 225).[17]

Yet it is not the Jewish aspiration to see the child make good in his studies that constitutes the chief object of criticism; neither does the plot of the story culminate in the school examination, but in the pogrom. The parallel structure of the plot invites the reader to seek a common denominator of the two traumas the boy suffers: the examination and the pogrom. This common denominator is the experience of encountering antisemitism.

The "victory" of the examination pass marks the first round. It is a false breakthrough since it fosters in the narrator and his family the illusion that the young generation, by being diligent and worthy, may gain admission into Russian society. And indeed the Jewish boy proves to his gentile teacher that he knows Russian history and literature better than gentile children and forces him, however grudgingly, to admire his accomplishments. This admiration, however, is couched in words with an antisemitic flavor: "'What a people', the old man whispered, 'these little Jews of yours! There's a devil in them'" (p. 222).

The illusion built up by the success in the examination reinforces the shock of the pogrom and its lack of any rational causality. It stresses the effect of total absurdity: "'Their spawn must be wiped out,' said Kate, ... 'I can't a-bear their spawn, nor their stinking menfolk'" (p. 230). David Roskies writes in his book *Against the Apocalypse* (Harvard, 1984): "Life, in Babel's scheme; was a series of initiations into violence" (p. 161). The plot structure of "The Story of My Dovecot" offers a visual model of this idea.

NOTES

4. All quotations taken from Isaac Babel, *Collected Stories*, trans. or revised by W. Morison (Harmondsworth, Middlesex, 1961).

17. The inversion of sexual roles in traditional Jewish society is particularly emphasized in another story by Babel, "The King," in the descriptions of the bride and groom. On this point he may have been influenced by Mendele Mocher Sforim.

—Hamutal Bar-Yosef, "On Isaac Babel's 'The Story of My Dovecot.'" *Prooftexts* 6, no. 3 (September 1986): pp. 265, 268–269.

ALICE STONE NAKHIMOVSKY ON MYTHMAKING

[Alice Stone Nakhimovsky is a Professor of Russian and Department Chair of Russian Studies at Colgate University. In addition to a number of published articles, she most notably wrote *Russian-Jewish Literature and Identity*.]

Babel's childhood stories are as different from the Odessa stories as they are from *Red Cavalry*. Though set in Odessa, they are neither hyperbolic nor broadly comic; their language is more muted and their contrasts more delicate. Unlike the stories of the other two cycles, these do not stake out new ground. Their premise is a familiar one, a journey back to the author's childhood. Their tone is emotional and, given Babel's brevity, introspective.

For Babel, as for other writers, this recreation of childhood is a type of mythmaking—the construction of a past that has an overriding psychological validity even if the details are made up. In Babel's case, the myth is that of the Jewish child whose experience reflects that of other Jewish children. "The Story of

My Dovecote" is characteristic: the narrator is held up as the archetypical Jew by those, Russians and Jews, who wish him well, by those who beat him up, and even in his own mind, "Like all Jews I was short and weakly and had headaches from studying."⁹⁹ Perhaps because of the importance of the Jewish theme to these stories, their narrator is more immersed in the Jewish world than Babel was. The narrator spends his early years "chained to the Talmud," which Babel did not; the narrator experiences a pogrom and the humiliation of his father, which Babel never did. But the contrast between Russian and Jew that runs through these stories and the desire to escape the Jewish world may be reasonably assumed to reflect a felt reality.

The images that adhere to Jews in the childhood stories are similar to images of Jews in *Red Cavalry*. Jews are not at home in the physical world; they are not robust or sexual. The stories "Story of My Dovecote" and "First Love" are about Jewish powerlessness, in part physical and sexual, as perceived by a young boy. (...)

With what do Jews fight back? In "The Story of My Dovecote," set during the same pogrom described in "First Love," they fight with intellect. Faced with severe restrictions on Jewish admission to secondary school, the narrator studies intensely for years; he memorizes books, crams himself with "every imaginable subject,"¹⁰⁴ and spews it forth at the exam in a blaze of self-forgetfulness. This triumph is described by the grown-up Jews who watch it as "the victory of David over Goliath."

It goes without saying that the victory does not stand. For one thing, it is undermined by the boy himself, who, while fulfilling his parents' desires and his own Jewish destiny, wants nothing so much as doves and a dovecote. Owning doves is suitable for Odessa rowdies, but it is an unexpected, Russian-oriented desire for this Jewish boy.¹⁰⁵ Doves are prized for their physical display and for their flight—how could he take possession of them? And of course he doesn't. David can win over Goliath only in the restricted atmosphere of a school exam. In the marketplace, caught in the pogrom, he and his doves are no match even for a Russian cripple.

Babel being Babel, this story is not without its contradictory overtones. First is the hint that the violent pogrom cleanses the narrator from the neurosis of his exams. There is a similarity to his experience in the heat of the exams and during the pogrom—in both cases, he is described as both "blind" and free of self-restraint. Pressed to the ground by the cripple, the blood of his doves smeared over him, he is able to cry freely. Second and more significant is the story of grandfather Shoil. Shoil is killed, but he does not hide; before he is killed he curses his assailants for all he is worth. The anecdote about Shoil is told to the narrator in the penultimate paragraphs of the story, and while it does not quite represent Jewish strength, it still sounds a note of resistance.

The character of Shoil brings into view another way of Jewish being that runs through these stories. The narrator's family includes not only frail and nervous Jews but also the occasional self-assertive one. To this category, in addition to Shoil, belong Uncle Lev the adventurer and the noisy madmen Leivi-Itskhok and Simon-Wolf from "The Awakening."[106]

NOTES

99. Babel', *Detstvo*, 40; Morison, 255.

104. Babel', *Detstvo*, 36; Morison, 252 ("every scrap of learning").

105. Note the dovecote—the "finest in town"—owned by the three tough blacksmith's sons in "Karl Yankel'" (Babel', Detstvo, 308; not in Morison). In Sholem Asch's *East River*, owning dogs is also seen as a rather un-Jewish endeavor. This does not cancel out the significant connotation of doves as symbols of peace.

106. As we saw in "First Love," Russians, but not Jews, had the freedom to assert themselves and act absurdly if they so desired. Here are self-assertive Jews who possess the freedom of absolute madness. The narrator is ashamed of his uncle's "noisy madness, full of mindless fire" (Babel', *Detstvo*, 61; missing in Morison).

> —Alice Stone Nakhimovsky, "Isaac Babel." In *Russian-Jewish Literature and Identity*. (Baltimore: John Hopkins University Press, 1992): pp. 102–3, 104–5.

EFRAIM SICHER ON ANTI-SEMITISM

[Efraim Sicher teaches at Ben-Gurion University of the Negev. He is the author of a book and several essays about Isaak Babel, and has edited three volumes of Babel's prose. His publications also cover a wide range of topics in comparative literature from Dickens and George Eliot to Arnold Wesker and dystopian fiction.]

A fellow Odessite, the Russian novelist Konstantin Paustovsky, attested to Babel's sensitivity to anti-Semitism by quoting him as saying, 'I didn't choose to be a Jew ... I am a Jew, a Yid. At times I think I can understand everything. But one thing I will never understand and that's the reason for that filthy treachery which goes by the humdrum name of anti-Semitism.'[29] The short story 'Story of My Dovecote' (1925) records the painful impression made by pogroms on the occasion of the 1905 Constitution. In the story which follows 'Story of My Dovecote', 'Pervaia liubov" ('First Love'), the boy joins his parents, who are sheltering at the house of their Russian neighbours, but cannot resolve the contradiction between the reality of his father debasing himself in the mud before a Cossack officer, while his own portrait is thrown out of his father's store, and the fantasy of his passion for the Russian Galina. In early editions the father is named 'Babel', thus emphasizing the split identity in the portrayal of the narrator.[30] Babel defamiliarizes that 'humdrum name' in order to render all the more effective its inhuman brutality and stupidity, and that is why the word 'pogrom' is mentioned only at the end of 'Story of My Dovecote'. Babel was one of the few Jewish authors to portray pogroms in Russian after the Revolution, besides Mikhail Kozakov ('The Man Who Prostrated Himself', 1930), the children's author Lev Kassil (*Shvambraniia*, 1933) and Aleksei Svirsky (*Story of My Life*, 1935). In 1930 Babel's 'Story of My Dovecote' was still being coopted by official Party propaganda against anti-Semitism, but gradually any mention that anti-Semitism still existed in Soviet Russia was prohibited.

Although Babel told Michael Gold in Paris in 1935 that there was no longer a 'Jewish Question' in Russia,[31] this is not borne out by his published writing. His 'Story of My Dovecote' leaves an unforgettable impression of what it meant for a Jewish boy in Tsarist Russia to grow up into the adult world of sexuality and violent pogroms. 'The Journey' and 'Beresteczko' describe the atrocities of the Civil War period. Rather than presenting a Marxist standpoint and portraying the pogrom as the work of reactionaries, as does Valentin Kataev in 'Lone White Sail' or Nikolai Ostrovsky in *How the Steel Was Tempered*, Babel depicts the violence done to Jews before and after the Revolution as their natural lot. In 'Story of My Dovecote' the cripple Makarenko, seeing he is getting nothing but bonnets from the looting, strikes the Jewish boy, squashing his newly purchased doves, a Biblical symbol of peace and sacrifice. His rage is matched by Katiusha's venom: 'Their seed should be wiped out ... I can't stand their seed and their stinking men' (45). The trauma threatens Jewish and sexual identity; but it is a formative, cathartic experience in the maturation of the artist, as in that of the boy in Joyce's 'Araby'.

NOTES

29. Konstantin Paustovsky, *Vremia bol'shikh ozhidanii* (Moscow, 1960), 151–2.

30. There is no evidence that the Babel family were harmed by the violent outbreaks of 1904–5, and it is denied by Nathalie Babel, *The Lonely Years 1925–1939: Unpublished Stories and Private Correspondence*, edited by Nathalie Babel (NY: Farrar, Strauss, & Co., 1964).

31. Michael Gold, 'A Love Letter from France', *New Masses*, 13 August 1935. This article was translated into Russian in *Literaturnyi Leningrad*, 14 September 1935, 1.

—Efraim Sicher, *Jews in Russian Literature After the October Revolution*. New York: Cambridge University Press, 1995: 79–80.

"The Awakening"

To establish his own social standing, the narrator of "The Awakening" first mentions how all people in his Jewish family's circle, "middlemen, storekeepers, clerks in banks and steamship offices," enroll their children in music lessons. These parents place their hopes and dreams on the shoulders of their children, knowing that they themselves will probably never achieve anything greater than middle-class status. The town of Odessa, in particular, embraces this line of thinking, having indeed produced a number of child prodigies. Mothers take their sons, at four or five years old, to Mr. Zagursky, who trawls the slums for music students. The boys first study with him, then, if they show promise, they are sent to Leopold Auer in Petersburg. The narrator reveals that he is too old to be a child prodigy—nearly fourteen—but that he could pass for an eight year old, thanks to his small stature, a source of perpetual self-consciousness for the Jewish boys and men who appear in Babel's prose. In this story, the narrator wryly notes that the deception regarding his age was where the family "lay all [their] hopes."

The narrator is brought to Mr. Zagursky, who agrees to a low price for his lessons out of respect for the boy's grandfather; the grandfather is the town joke but also its pride, since, in a top hat and ragged shoes, he answers any question asked of him, no matter what the topic. Through reference to this character, readers see the first hint of the narrator's potential to rebel, since a man within his own family has already chosen a truly unconventional path. But the boy, for the time being, goes to his lessons, and Zagursky expends much effort into training the boy, to no avail; he is a terrible player, though his father refuses to give up. He and his family talk about the successes of other Odessa children often, and though his father is resigned to living in poverty, he desires fame. He takes others out to dine, and they re-emphasize the idea that there's no way the grandson of such a man would live in obscurity. Again, the reference to the grandfather as the source of the boy's talent links him with the old man more palpably, and the description of both the father and grandfather work to fulfill the criteria of typical Babelian men: they live more in their minds and imagination more than they do in the tangible world around them.

The narrator, meanwhile, admits to being distracted himself, reading books by Dumas and Turgenev on his music stand while practicing. He tells stories to neighborhood boys during the day and writes stories down each night, remarking that this penchant for writing is hereditary. His Grandpa Levy-Itskhok had spent his life writing a novel called *The Headless Man*, and the narrator believes he is following in his footsteps. But with his violin and sheet music, he drags himself to Zagursky's, seeing Jewish mothers holding on to violins nicer than those "destined to play at Buckingham Palace." He watches children leave and enter, and thinks of Zagursky's red curls, bow tie, and thin legs. The boy decides he shouldn't be there then, recognizing that his ancestors have called him to a different vocation.

This longing to escape the seemingly tightly circumscribed, closed-off world of Jewish values and goals runs as a thread through much of Babel's work, often demonstrating how self-loathing externally gains expression. In this case, however, the narrator simply has enough self-awareness to identify his own strengths and weaknesses; because they conflict with the prescribed course of action for success, he must rebel against the status quo, making the story a miniaturized version of James Joyce's *Portrait of the Artist as a Young Man*.

The narrator states that the choice to revolt was difficult, but one day, armed with his instrument, music, and the money for a month's worth of lessons, he turns down a different street (literally and figuratively), and finds himself at the port. He stays there for three hours, and never sees Zagursky's waiting room again, claiming that he is filling his head with more important things. He and a classmate, Nemanov, get in the habit of boarding a particular boat and talking to an old sailor called Mr. Trottyburn. Though Nemanov is a year younger than the narrator, he is a prodigy in business and trade, and the narrator notes that he later becomes a New York millionaire, a general manager for General Motors. At port, he brings the narrator along because he follows instructions, and Nemanov soon begins trading in smuggled tobacco pipes, made by Trottyburn's brother.

Trottyburn notably refers to hand-made pipes as children: "The one thing [my brother] believes in is that you have to make your children with your own hands, you can't leave that sort of thing to others." Nemanov sells them to the wealthy at one hundred percent profit, and the narrator notes the skilled craftsmanship invested in the pipes, imagining their maker living in old England.

The waves, the narrator tells us, separate him from his "home reeking of onions and Jewish fate," emphasizing his remove from the insularity and expectations of his family. From the harbor, he moves to the breakwater, where local boys swim, dive under fishing boats, steal coconuts, and wait for watermelon carts to come by. The narrator yearns to learn how to swim, though he's ashamed that he never saw the water until he was ten. He reflects, with regret, on how he learned essential things late in life, but when he tries to learn how to swim, he fails. "The hydrophobia of my ancestors, the Spanish rabbis and Frankfurt money changers, dragged me to the bottom." Significantly, he blames his Jewish ancestry for his failures, just as he says that genetics are to blame for his storytelling penchant. Though he is rebelling from the proscribed path for young Jews in Odessa, he nonetheless still feels that his gifts, as well as his flaws, all stem from his identity as a Jew. So the boy's failure in swimming persists until a proofreader for the *Odessa News*, Efim Nikitich Smolich, who had a "warmth for Jewish boys," arrives, playing with them often on the beach.

This man has a powerful, erotically-charged appeal for the narrator, as readers should note from Babel's description: "He lay among us by the breakwater, the king of these melon and kerosene waters, with his copper shoulders, his head that of an aging gladiator, and his lightly crooked, bronze legs. I loved him as only a boy afflicted with hysteria and headaches can love an athlete. I didn't leave his side, and tried to please him every way I could." Jewish self-loathing seeps through this statement, as the narrator views himself as weak and un-masculine, while the journalist—presumably non-Jewish, since his affection for "Jewish boys" is so pointedly emphasized—is everything that the boy is not, and therefore ideal.

Nikitich urges the narrator to calm himself when trying to swim, and soon the man invites the boy to his garret, which was unusual. The man showed the boy his animals, and the boy, in return, showed him a tragedy (notably, by definition, a story in which the narrator causes his own downfall) that he had written just the night before. The man, after remarking that he suspected the boy of being a writer because he was "no longer looking at things," reads the work, paces, and states that he sees a "divine spark" in the boy. They go into the street, and Nikitich says that there's something missing from the boy's work, finally identifying it as a lack of knowledge about the natural world. The man points at trees, bushes, and birds, asking the boy to identify them, which he can't. This causes a huge shift in the boy's perspective, making him grounded and aware of the tangible world around him, as opposed to the Babelian man-in-training who always has his head in the clouds. Nikitich remarks to him that no writer would compose anything worthwhile without such knowledge, blaming the boy's parents for this failure. The boy, without speaking, thinks that his parents were struggling to get by, day to day.

At dinner that night, at home, the boy can't eat, reflecting on Nikitich's words. He struggles to think of who could teach him this knowledge, as well as what he might already know, when his father starts to tell a story about Jascha Heifetz, who is currently making eight hundred rubles a performance; through such means, the father re-emphasizes his hopes and dreams for his son. The boy does the math to figure how much this comes to a month when he looks out the window and sees the music teacher, Mr. Zagursky, coming through the yard. Three months have passed since the boy tossed the violin into the water. He rushed to the back door as the music teacher approached the front, but the back had been boarded up the night before to prevent break-ins, so he locked himself in the bathroom.

Within a half hour, the whole family had gathered around the bathroom door, the women crying, the father silent until he said,

"I am an officer.... I have an estate. I ride out on hunts. The muzhiks pay me rent. I sent my son to the Cadet Corps. There is no reason for me to lose any sleep over my son." After a quiet moment, the father begins to throw his body against the door, repeating some of the words again, until only the bolt holds the door on, attached by a single nail. (This violent response to the shattering of the father's dreams echoes a scene in "The Story of My Dovecote," wherein the father, after learning that his son was cheated out of a spot at the Lycée because of a bribe, wished to beat up the man who paid the money.) The women grab at the father's legs, and the father's mother enters. Speaking in Yiddish, she tells him that though their family's sorrow was great, she didn't want to see blood in this house. The boy hears the father walk away and stays in the bathroom until nightfall. The boy's aunt then takes the boy to his grandmother's, and as they walk, he notes the shrubs and trees and birds that he can't identify, thus demonstrating that his perspective is already permanently altered, and he wonders about constellations and the machinations of the universe. His aunt holds his hand tightly, so he can't run away, and he admits that she's right to do so—that he'd thought of doing that very thing. Of course, intellectually speaking, he has already fled his family, but his compunction to escape his family and their expectations still persists on a psychological level.

LIST OF CHARACTERS IN

"The Awakening"

The narrator is a small-bodied fourteen-year-old Jewish boy living in Odessa, where Jewish families have collectively latched onto the dream of their children becoming musical prodigies. The narrator is more inclined toward writing stories than performing music, however, and starts to skip his scheduled violin lessons with Mr. Zagursky to spend time at the docks. There, he meets Efim Nikitich Smolich, a newspaperman who not only encourages the boy's writing, but makes him realize that his ignorance of the natural world will prevent him from ever being a good writer. This makes the narrator focus on his surroundings more intently, searching for the names of things, even while in the midst of crisis, such as when his heartbroken family learns of his deception.

The narrator's father, like the father in "The Story of My Dovecote," pins all his hopes for the family's success and happiness on his son. He talks often about Odessa kids who got their start in music with Zagursky and now get large sums of money for each performance. When Zagursky finally comes to the family's home to report the narrator's truancy, the father is furious and miserable, nearly breaking down the bathroom door to reach his hiding son.

The narrator's grandfather is Odessa's pride as well as the town joke. He is mad, wandering the streets in a top hat and ragged shoes, but he has answers to every question asked of him. It is out of respect for this grandfather that Mr. Zagursky arranges for the narrator to take violin lessons at a great discount.

Mr. Zagursky is the music teacher who trains the young children of Odessa, sending the best musicians on to Petersburg to further their studies. He comes to the narrator's home toward the end of the story to report his truancy.

Efim Nikitich Smolich is a newspaperman who has an affinity with young Jewish boys, and he spends much time with them down by the docks. The narrator quickly comes to idolize him, latching on to him and seeking him out for praise and validation. The boy eventually shows Nikitich a story that he wrote, and the man encourages him, but tells him that he must learn the names of everything that surrounds him—flowers, trees, bushes, and other natural phenomena.

Mr. Trottyburn is a sailor who smuggles wood-carved tobacco pipes that his expatriate brother makes by hand. The narrator and his friend, Nemanov, befriend the man, and soon Nemanov begins to sell the pipes, making a huge profit.

Nemanov, though younger than the narrator, is more worldly. Through sales of Trottyburn's smuggled, hand-made pipes, he makes large profits, foreshadowing his successful future in America as a general manager of General Motors.

"The Awakening"

LIONEL TRILLING ON EDUCATION

[Lionel Trilling was an American critic, author, and Professor of English at Columbia University. His essays—collected as *The Liberal Imagination*, *The Opposing Self*, *A Gathering of Fugitives*, and *Beyond Culture*—combine social, psychological, and political insights with literary criticism and scholarship. Other works include a novel, *Middle of the Journey*; *Matthew Arnold*, a pioneering use of Freudian psychology in analyzing a public figure and his work, *E. M. Forster*; *The Life and Work of Sigmund Freud*; and *Sincerity and Authenticity*.]

Babel spoke with bitterness of the terrible discipline of his Jewish education. He thought of the Talmud Torah as a prison shutting him off from all desirable life, from reality itself. One of the stories he tells—perhaps the incident was invented to stand for his feelings about his Jewish schooling—is about his father's having fallen prey to the Messianic delusion which beset the Jewish families of Odessa, the belief that any one of them might produce a prodigy of the violin, a little genius who could be sent to be processed by Professor Auer in Petersburg, who would play before crowned heads in a velvet suit, and support his family in honor and comfort. Such miracles occurred in Odessa, whence came Elman, Zimbalist, and Heifetz. Babel's father hoped for wealth, but he would have forgone wealth if he could have peen sure, at a minimum, of fame. Being small, the young Babel at fourteen might pass for eight and a prodigy. In point of fact, Babel had not even talent, and certainly no vocation. He was repelled by the idea of becoming a musical "dwarf," one of the "big-headed freckled children with necks as thin as flower stalks and an epileptic flush on their cheeks." This was a Jewish fate and he fled from it, escaping to the port and the beaches of Odessa.

Here he tried to learn to swim and could not: "the hydrophobia of my ancestors—Spanish rabbis and Frankfurt moneychangers —dragged me to the bottom." But a kindly proofreader, an elderly man who loved nature and children, took pity on him. "How d'you mean, the water won't hold you? Why shouldn't it hold you?"—his specific gravity was no different from anybody else's and the good Yefim Nikitich Smolich taught him to swim. "I came to love that man," Babel says in one of the very few of his sentences over which no slightest irony plays, "with the love that only a boy suffering from hysteria and headaches can feel for a real man."

The story is called "Awakening" and it commemorates the boy's first effort of creation. It is to Nikitich that he shows the tragedy he has composed and it is the old man who observes that the boy has talent but no knowledge of nature and who undertakes to teach him how to tell one tree or one plant from another. This ignorance of the natural world—Babel refers to it again in his autobiographical sketch—was a Jewish handicap to be overcome. It was not an extravagance of Jewish self-consciousness that led him to make the generalization—Maurice Samuel remarks in *The World of Sholom Aleichem* that in the Yiddish vocabulary of the Jews of eastern Europe there are but two flower names (rose, violet) and no names for wild birds.

—Lionel Trilling, "Isaac Babel," *Beyond Culture*. New York: Viking, 1965: pp. 132–33.

PATRICIA CARDEN ON INTELLECTUALISM

[Patricia Carden is the Director of Undergraduate Studies at Cornell University, where she teaches Russian literature. Her book, *The Art of Isaac Babel*, was one of the first comprehensive works of Babel scholarship in English, providing a thorough textual analysis of most of his work; the book remains a touchstone in the field.]

"Awakening" is among the most popular of Babel's stories. It shares with that other popular story, "The Death of Dolgushov," a deceptive transparency that pleases the reader and gives him to understand that at last he knows what the story is about. In these stories Babel comes closest to the conventional surface of his subjects and presents them in their most palatable forms: killing as an act of mercy, repression as the rather comic and familiar story of the little boy who is forced to take violin lessons. To the extent that "Awakening" can be received as the conventional story it is unsatisfactory, for it conceals the anguished travail leading to understanding at the very time that it benefits from it for its point. In Babel's other stories, even in the other stories of the childhood cycle, the style preserves the tension of the creative act. We feel the cost involved not as clumsiness but as a peculiar brilliance and power that set the stories apart from other stories. In "Awakening" there is a relaxation of tension. No doubt this benign style comes from Babel's own sense of ease with the materials now that he has reached understanding through the writing of the earlier stories. Seen in the context of the cycle the story gains, for we see how we arrive at this tranquility and transcendence.

"Awakening" takes its place in the cycle by showing the boy's grasp of another facet of reality, the sensuous nature of the world. The story basks in the radiance of the Southern landscape, resurrected for the first time since the Odessa stories. As in "In the Basement," the child's bookishness cuts him off from a direct, physical relationship to the world. The barrier that study creates between the boy and real life is symbolized in the hated violin lessons, another instrument of the father's ambitions. His father hopes that the son will be a prodigy, as so many other Odessa Jewish children have been, and thus bring glory to the family.

In his discussion of the story, Lionel Trilling calls attention to the ignorance of the natural world that was typical of the Jews of the eastern ghettos.[6] It is touching to find Babel writing in his diary of the Polish campaign, "I am learning the names of plants." Babel displaces this fact back into childhood and makes a good Russian the "teacher" who reveals this knowledge to the boy. Old Nikitich, the true master who will educate the boy to his vocation of writing, is opposed to the false master, the violin teacher. Nikitich reads the boy's first literary effort, a tragedy, and advises him to acquire a greater knowledge of the natural world. "A man who doesn't live in nature like a stone or an animal won't write two lasting lines in his whole life."

The moment inevitably comes when the father discovers that the boy has been shirking his violin lessons. His rage is appropriate to a man who has had his life's dream torn from him. The boy locks himself in the toilet, where he hears his father outside the door recounting, in an insanely calm voice, a formula from his life of fantasy: "'I am an officer,' my father said. 'I own an estate. I go hunting. The peasants pay me rent. I place my son in the cadet corps. I don't have to worry about my son.'" Aunt Bobka smuggles the boy out of the house to save him from his father's wrath. As the two fugitives advance along the street, the boy has an acute sense of the physical reality of the world. The story ends, "I thought of escape."

"Awakening" has a special significance in the cycle, for it reveals more clearly than any other story why the child "had to go through all that." The meaning of his ordeal lies in his future vocation. Babel gives here a portrait of the artist as a very young man. Each episode reveals the impact on the individual sensibility of a growing awareness of life's choices.

NOTE

6. Introduction to *The Collected Stories*, p. 24.

—Patricia Carden, *The Art of Isaac Babel.* Ithaca Cornell University Press, 1972: pp. 175–77.

JAMES E. FALEN ON ART AND NATURE

[James E. Falen, Professor of Russian at the University of Tennessee, wrote *Isaac Babel, Russian Master of the Short Story*, an important, comprehensive addition to Babel scholarship in English, as well as a translation of Pushkin's *Eugene Onegin.*]

Although the Jews of Odessa had a sense of belonging to the community and were able to participate in its energetic life, the stigma of the ghetto remained, and Babel is often bitter in speaking of his youth. Raymond Rosenthal, who has written an impressive appreciation of Babel, comments on Babel's reaction to ghetto life:

> Most accounts of his youth contain as a running theme this urge to escape from the ghetto. But this wish was hardly unique with Babel. Under the buffeting of the great social storms of the late 19th and early 20th centuries in Russia, the ghetto stood in a particularly exposed position. All the fury of aroused reaction was directed at its inhabitants, as though to warn them against the social transformation for which they longed. Yet in Babel, the impulse to escape took a contradictory form. While trying to throw off the hermetic restraints of the ghetto, he was still unable to rid himself of its molding influences. Throughout his writings it is this conflict between the ineradicable imprint of his Jewish heritage and his passionate wish to rise out of its circumscribed environment that imparts a lyrical tension to his prose.... For him, the cultural walls of Jewish life had become an obstacle to his most poignant aims.[15]

And what were these most poignant aims whose promise seemed to lie outside the ghetto walls, outside the limits of Jewish experience? In "The Awakening," a story that is central to an understanding of his life and art, Babel tells of some of his frustrated aspirations at thirteen: his desire to escape from the Jewish destiny implied by his father's wish to make him a child prodigy on the violin and his longing instead to learn to swim, to understand nature, and to write. The story is a metaphorical picture of two worlds: the closed Jewish life of his forebears, of "freaks" and "dwarfs" as he calls the musical prodigies, and the world of Efim Nikitich Smolich, proofreader of the *Odessa News*, suntanned athlete and idol of the local children. When Babel escapes from his music lessons to the port, it is to Nikitich that he runs, to the man who, like a father, can teach him to swim, who will criticize his youthful writings and encourage him to develop a feeling for nature. The yearnings attributed here to his childhood are reenacted by Babel in various guises throughout his maturity, and their expression becomes a recurring motif throughout his writing.

But "The Awakening" suggests an even deeper and more unattainable desire, one hidden from Babel himself. At times he seems to wish that art and nature become one. The lack of experience that so torments him is invariably expressed in intellectual and aesthetic terms. The boy discovers that he lacks knowledge of nature, that he does not know the names for plants and birds. The implication is not that he will give up writing in order to experience nature, but that he will learn to put nature into art. Insofar as this means endowing the word with the weight of experience, it is no more than that essential ingredient of art sought by all writers. But Babel seems to make no distinction between the living of an experience and its aesthetic reincarnation. He desires simultaneously both to express and to possess, and this effort at making art itself into experience, this attempt to conjoin the aesthetic and the sensual, is one of Babel's most lasting struggles.

NOTE

15. Raymond Rosenthal, "The Fate of Isaac Babel," *Commentary* (Feb. 1947), 127–28.

—James E. Falen, *Isaac Babel, Russian Master of the Short Story.* Knoxville: University of Tennessee, 1974: pp. 11–13.

EFRAIM SICHER ON GHETTO MENTALITY

[Efraim Sicher teaches at Ben-Gurion University of the Negev. He is the author of a book and several essays about Isaak Babel, and has edited three volumes of Babel's prose. His publications also cover a wide range of topics in comparative literature from Dickens and George Eliot to Arnold Wesker and dystopian fiction.]

In Babel's stories the narrator constantly seeks to escape the stifling confines of his native Jewish world, its ghetto mentality enforced by the territorial, economic and social restrictions of the Pale of Settlement. This theme of flight from the *shtetl*, from the traditional Jewish community, is a favorite theme of Jewish literature following the nineteenth-century secular Jewish enlightenment (*Haskala*), but so often there is nowhere safe and secure to run to, as the Novograd-Volynsk novelist M. Z. Feierberg indicated, despite the Zionist solution, in the title of his *Whither?* (1899). The Jew who has broken from his roots inside the Jewish home remains an outsider with no place in gentile society.

Just as the youth in Bialik's *Beyond the Fence* is drawn to the realm of nature, to the gentile Marinka beyond the forbidden fence, in Babel's childhood story "Awakening" the boy yearns to flee beyond closed boundaries into the open space of the non-Jewish world, to abandon his violin for the lessons of nature:

> V detstve, prigvozhdennyi k Gemare, ya vel zhizn' mudretsa, vyrosshi—stal lazat' po derev'yam.

> As a child nailed to the Gemara I led the life of a sage, when I grew up I started climbing trees.*

The boy is fighting the hydrophobia induced, according to him, along with bookishness and emotional hysteria, by the indoor urban Jewish life; he wants to swim, to break out of the tradition *enclosed* Jewish world into the unfamiliar non-Jewish world of nature *outside*.

NOTE

Isaak Babel, Detstuo; drugie rasskazy, ed, Efraim Sicher (Jerusalem: Biblioteka Aliya, 1979), p. 71.

—Efraim Sicher, *Style and Structure in the Prose of Isaak Babel.* Columbus: Slavica, 1986: p. 86.

PLOT SUMMARY OF

"Guy de Maupassant"

At the story's outset, the unnamed narrator states that it is 1916 in Petersburg, and he has forged papers and no money. Aleksei Kazantsev, a Russian philology teacher, provides the narrator with a place to stay. Kazantsev does Spanish translations for extra money, and although he's never been to Spain, he passionately loves the idea of the country, and this makes him happy. People down on their luck often gravitate toward Kazantsev, and the narrator, looking to place an occasional article in the press, like others in the teacher's company, trawls the morgues and police stations each morning. In November, the narrator receives a job offer to be a clerk in a factory, which would exclude him from conscription, but he refuses, saying he would never work as a clerk. At twenty, the narrator vows that he would rather go hungry than be a lackey. This establishes the narrator as an idealistic young man who sees the world in black and white terms, and who embraces the romanticized tenets of bohemianism.

At Christmas, a lawyer named Bendersky, who owns Halcyon Publishing House, decides to release new editions of Guy de Maupassant's works, translated by his wife, Raisa. Kazantsev recommends the story's narrator to Bendersky for the task of helping with the stalled translations, and the next day, wearing another man's jacket, the narrator arrives at the Bendersky's home. It is gaudy in its overdone splendor, and the narrator notes that this was common for Jewish bankers who converted to Christianity and felt the need to overcompensate for their lack "family" and "breeding." In this instance, instead of self-loathing on the part of the narrator, we see it manifested in other characters—specifically, the rich. Clearly, by way of showy furnishings, homes, clothes, and jewelry, in addition to an outright denouncement of their religion and culture, these characters are trying desperately to make themselves into a perceived ideal, and thus reject all that they are by nature. Babel presents his readers again, by way of the Benderskys, depictions of Jewish characters who view themselves through the anti-Semitic eyes of those around them.

The Benderskys live on the third floor, and the door is opened by a maid who leads the narrator into the living room. The Slavic decor doesn't distract him from watching the maid move around the room; she is nearsighted, indolent, well built, and haughty, the narrator tells us—not a striking beauty—but then he says, "I thought how she must thrash about with savage agility when she made love." This seems surprising, but the narrator's young age is relevant to his prurient interests, thus reminding readers not only that he is just out of adolescence, but also that his imagination makes high drama of all things. The curtain over the door opens to reveal Raisa—black hair, pink eyes, and large breasts. The narrator remarks that she must be one of a "ravishing breed of Jewesses from Kiev or Poltava," noting that these women tend to fatten up their bodies with their husbands' money, but that they also drive men crazy.

Raisa tells the narrator that Maupassant is the single passion of her life, and then she leaves the room to get her translation of "Miss Harriet," struggling to keep her hips from swinging. The narrator notes that Raisa's translation lacked the author's "free-flowing prose with its powerful breath of passion." She translated meticulously and correctly, but without any sense of style, "the way Jews in the past used to write Russian." (Her translation style, of course, suggests that Raisa, like her translation, has lacked passion in her life; she has done what was expected of her, but her life lacked beauty.) The narrator takes the translation home with him that evening, editing it liberally in Kazantsev's attic. He says that the task isn't as bad as it might appear: "When a phrase is born, it is both good and bad at the same time. The secret of its success rests in a crux that is barely discernible. One's fingertips must grasp the key, gently warming it. And then the key must be turned once, not twice." Here, and throughout, Babel writes about the process of writing, and tells a story about two readers' interaction with fictional stories, making "Guy de Maupassant" a metaliterary text.

The next morning, the narrator brings the edited manuscript to Raisa and reads it aloud to her as she sits, transfixed, with her hands clasped together. She comes undone as she listens, however, marveling at the young man's skill. He replies, "I spoke to her of style, of an army of words, an army in which every type of weapon is deployed. No iron spike can pierce a human heart as icily as a period in the right place." Language, depicted as violent and militaristic in the mind of the narrator, gives way then to sexuality, as Babel describes Raisa's provocative posture, her parted lips, and her stockinged legs, spread apart. And of course, in this moment of intense sexual awareness and need, the maid, while avoiding the narrator's and Raisa's eyes, brings in breakfast on a tray. Violence and sex are thus significantly juxtaposed, with one seemingly leading to the other in the narrator's mind.

The sunlight, coming through the windows, touches the twenty-nine Maupassant books that stand on a shelf above a table, and as Raisa and the narrator drink coffee from small cups, they begin work on "Idyll." (The tale involves a young carpenter who drinks milk from the breasts of a fat wet-nurse while traveling by train from Nice to Marseilles, an image that seems to resonate with the image readers have of the buxom Raisa working with the narrator.) The narrator leaves the Benderskys with an advance, which he spends on fine food and drink for himself and his compatriots at Karantsev's. Drunk, the narrator starts to rail against Tolstoy, claiming that fear made him turn to religion. He and the others fall asleep on the floor, and the narrator has erotic dreams about Katya, the middle-aged washerwoman who lives in the story below. The next morning, however, when he goes to get boiling water from her, he's disappointed by the reality of a plain, aging woman. This small moment is a precursor for what follows; reality can only fail to live up to the young man's imagination.

The narrator breakfasts, from then on, at the Benderskys, and he and Raisa twice drive out to the islands. He tells her of his childhood, and this affects her. He's met her husband, who has the wandering eyes of a madman, thanks to profits made from military supplies, very likely against his own kind (again, self-loathing taken to an extreme). Raisa is embarrassed to introduce him to new people, and the narrator explains that because of his youth, he didn't understand this at first. This emphasizes the distance from which the story is being narrated. Rather than experiencing it as it happens, we are viewing the story as the older, more experienced narrator now processes and interprets it.

Raisa's two sisters from Kiev visit after the first of the year. The narrator comes with his translation of "The Confession," but, not finding Raisa, he returns in the evening to hear a raucous din coming from the dining room, noting: "Dining is invariably boisterous in wealthy houses that lack pedigree. Their boisterousness was Jewish, with peals of thunder and melodious flourishes." In this passage, of course, it's not just the rich Jews whom the narrator views as crass, but the Jews' spiritedness in general that seems worthy of contempt, thus demonstrating that the narrator suffers from self-loathing himself as well, albeit in smaller doses than the Benderskys. Raisa soon comes to him, wearing a backless ball gown with showy jewelry, and comments on her own drunkenness. She sways, shakes her head, and falls into an armchair with "ancient Russian carving," subtly privileging Russian culture once again. Women's laughter sounds from the dining room again, and the sisters appear—tall, black-haired, and large-breasted like Raisa, also married to Benderskys. This set of neatly arranged, conventional marriages flies in the face of the narrator's bohemianism, of course, demonstrating the chasm that exists between their priorities and values and the young man's idealism. The women's husbands soon help them into coats and boots, trying to get to the opera.

Sometime later, Raisa tells the narrator she wants to work, regretting the loss of a week. As she brings a bottle of wine and two glasses from the dining room, he notes that her breasts are "loose in the silken sack of her dress" and that "her nipples stiffened, the silk impeding them," demonstrating again the young man's fixation on sex. Raisa tells the narrator that the wine is excellent, and that her husband will be angry at its being squandered, hinting at the first step toward her rebellion. The narrator polishes off three glasses, feeling drunk, and Raisa asks about their current translation project, "The Confession." The story involves a coachman, Polyte, who drives red-haired Céleste into town twice a week in order for her to sell her wares. Each time, Polyte crassly propositions her, she refuses, and he, red from laughing, tells her that it will happen someday.

The narrator then drinks another glass of wine, clinks glasses with Raisa, and the maid, that vessel of potentially wild sexuality, skulks through the room.

In "The Confession," after Céleste and Polyte have this flirtatious exchange for nearly two years, Céleste finally answers the coachman's initial question by saying, "I'm at your service, Monsieur Polyte." Raisa laughs and falls over the table, and then the focus shifts back to Maupassant's story again. The narrator notes that the buggy was driven by a white nag with "lips pink with age," and that the horse walked while the sun shone down on the vehicle, isolated from the world by its faded brown cover.

Raisa hands the narrator a fifth glass of wine, proposing a toast to Maupassant. The narrator uses the same line on her that Polyte used on Céleste, and he kisses her. She tells him he's funny, then presses her body back against a wall, spreading her arms, causing the narrator to remark, "Of all the gods ever crucified, she was the most captivating." This would appear to mock the Christianity to which Raisa and her husband have hollowly converted, as well as re-emphasizing the narrator's hyperbolic sense of drama. Raisa, calling the narrator "Monsieur Polyte," asks him to take a seat, which he does, only to jump up and cause the chair, and the twenty-nine Maupassant books on the shelf, to fall. This seems to suggest that the physical reality will once again fall short of the artful imagination. But as the narrator comments, "the white nag of my fate walked a slow walk," readers should be reminded that a white nag pulled Céleste and Polyte along as they made love, indicating that although Raisa and the narrator had previously been translating the Maupassant story's words, they were now trying to translate the story's content into their lives and make art into reality.

The narrator leaves after eleven, shortly before Raisa's husband and sisters are due back from the theater. Though sober, he weaves and sings gibberish while walking along the streets. Eerily, however, fog permeates the "tunnels of streets," and the narrator says, "Monsters roared behind seething walls." When he reaches home, he finds Kazantsev sleeping, sitting up, his blond hair (compared to "canary down," bringing up bird imagery in yet another Babel story) ruffled. He had been reading a 1624 edition of *Don Quixote*, with a dedication to Duke de Broglio on the title page. Here again, through characters reading, Babel establishes how fictional texts interact with human lives. In this case, the narrator can be viewed as a version of Don Quixote, a man trying to act in alignment with his ideals, to which he holds fast, and which compose his sense of himself in the world. The narrator lies down and pulls the lamp toward him to read Edouard de Maynial's biography of Maupassant.

The narrator learns that Maupassant contracted syphilis at age twenty-five, then suffered for years through worsening symptoms until, at age forty, he slit his throat. He survived the attempted suicide, though, and was placed in a madhouse. Reportedly, Maupassant crawled about on all fours while institutionalized, eating his own excrement. A last medical report stated that the author was degenerating into an animal state; Maupassant died at age forty-two. The reality of sexual disease, in conflict with the romanticism that surrounds Maupassant, stuns the narrator into reflection. The potential results of living life in the manner of fictional characters thus becomes problematic. The narrator finishes the biography and gets up from the bed, watching the fog at his window. The story ends with the narrator saying, "My heart constricted. I was touched by the premonition of truth." In this moment, the narrator's recognition of art's relation to reality shifts, such that their perfect conflagration is no longer something for which to strive; instead, the ring of truth that the narrator hears very likely brings back his disappointing experience with the washerwoman, Katya, and he realizes that art and reality, by necessity, serve different functions in human lives. As critic Charles Rougle noted, the story's young narrator ultimately finds that art is not simply a product of beauty, but also one of "pain, suffering, and burden of heredity."

"Guy de Maupassant"

The narrator is a young man who embraces the ideals and lifestyles of Bohemia. He eschews nine to five jobs and moves into an apartment shared by many of his ilk, though it officially belongs to a translator named Aleksei Kazantsev. Through Kazantsev, the narrator learns about an opportunity to work on translations of all of Guy de Maupassant's works. The publisher's wife, Raisa, works closely with the narrator on the project, and the two begin an affair.

Alexsei Kazantsev, a Russian philology teacher, also lives the bohemian lifestyle, opening his home to various writers and artists. To earn extra income, he translates Spanish works into Russian, and when he hears that a lawyer named Bendersky, who also owns a publishing house, wants to have Maupassant's works translated, he recommends the narrator for the task.

Bendersky is a lawyer—formerly Jewish, before converting to Christianity—and owner of a publishing house. He tries hard to fit into Russian aristocratic society, despite anti-Semitism and the prejudice against "new" money. The narrator notes, throughout the story, how the Bendersky home is furnished so decadently as to be considered garish, suggesting that the Benderskys, in general, try *too* hard to achieve an image of success. But despite all his financial success, Bendersky seems slightly mad, the result, the narrator speculates, of profiting from selling military supplies used against Jews during the war.

Raisa is from a family of large, vivacious Jewish women, many of whom have also married Benderskys. When the narrator first starts working with her on the Maupassant translations, he notes that her previous work on the project showed meticulous care in terms of correctness, but that the beauty of Maupassant's language and his flowing style had vanished. One night, when Bendersky goes to the opera with Raisa's sisters and their husbands, Raisa opens a bottle of expensive wine for the narrator and her to drink while they work on a translation of "The Confession," and after they both get drunk, they act out the sexual proposition found in the story.

The Bendersky's maid is a sturdy, haughty, nearsighted woman, always skulking in and out of the room where Raisa and the narrator work. Upon first seeing her, the narrator considers how wild she would likely be in bed.

Katya is a washerwoman who lives downstairs from Kazantsev. One night, the narrator has erotic dreams about her, but when he goes to get boiling water from her the next morning, he is disappointed by the sight of a plain, aging woman.

Polyte is a character in the Maupassant story, "The Confession." A coachman, he drives a redheaded woman named Céleste to the market twice a week for two years, always propositioning her by saying, "When are we going to have a bit of fun, ma belle?" Céleste refuses each time, which makes Polyte laugh and say, "We'll have fun someday, ma belle!"

Céleste is the woman in the Maupassant story, "The Confession," who refuses Polyte's advances. After two years, however, she surprises him by one day responding, "I'm at your service, M'sieur Polyte," and they make love in the coach.

CRITICAL VIEWS ON

"Guy de Maupassant"

PATRICIA CARDEN ON ILLUSION

[Patricia Carden is the Director of Undergraduate
Studies at Cornell University, where she teaches Russian
literature. Her book, *The Art of Isaac Babel*, was one of
the first comprehensive works of Babel scholarship in
English, providing a thorough textual analysis of most of
his work; the book remains a touchstone in the field.]

Babel continually widens the range of what can be held together
in the bounds of contemplation. In his fine late story "Guy de
Maupassant" he extends his concern to finding the just
relationship between our illusions and the truth of life about us.
Thus we are led through a series of events and observations
whose order is determined by, whose unity is found in, the act of
contemplation. The story presents us with one character after
another who lives in illusion: Kazantsev, whose world is Spain
and the Quixote; Benderski, who is mad from the profits he has
made on war supplies; Raissa, whose only passion is Maupassant.
Babel's young narrator, the same mythologized image of himself
as a young provincial storming Petersburg that figures in his
autobiographical sketches, lives entirely in his illusions. He sees
himself as a young Maupassant, sensual, touched by genius,
invincible. Constant reminders of mortality appear before him,
but he is oblivious to them.

The story reaches the climax of illusion as the narrator,
presumably having seduced Raissa, leaves the Benderski house.
The whole world becomes an extension of his fantasy,
frightening but exhilarating. "I swayed from side to side, singing
in a language I had just made up. In the tunnels of the streets,
hung with chains of lights, the steamy fog billowed. Monsters
roared behind the boiling walls. The roads amputated the legs of
those walking on them." This is the moment of freedom
celebrated by Babel in other stories, when the world is rendered

fluid by the imagination and the spirit in its power takes up its song in an unknown tongue. But in this story Babel presses farther. There remains a revelation beyond the revelation of freedom, and that is the revelation of necessity. The narrator comes, as at last he must come, back to his attic. There sits Kazantsev, plunged into sleep over his 1624 edition of *Don Quixote*, forever dead to the world. The narrator too picks up a book; but if books can be an escape from the world, they can also be a path by which we enter more fully into the truth of the world. Thus the narrator learns from Edouard Maynial's book on Maupassant the one thing he had not taken into account when choosing Maupassant as his guide in life:

> At twenty-five he experienced the first attack of congenital syphilis. The productivity and *joie de vivre* which were characteristic of him resisted the disease. At first he suffered from headaches and attacks of hypochondria. Then the specter of blindness rose before him. His vision weakened. He developed a suspicion of everyone, wanted to be alone, became quarrelsome. He struggled furiously, dashed around the Mediterranean in a yacht, fled to Tunis, Morocco, Central Africa. He continued writing constantly. Having attained fame, he cut his throat at the age of forty. He lost blood, but survived. He was locked up in a madhouse. There he crawled about on his hands and knees devouring his own excrement.[13] The last entry on his hospital report reads: "Monsieur de Maupassant va s'animaliser."

The author does not make a more explicit statement of the narrator's final discovery, but we see that he has at last been struck by the knowledge of mortality that he has successfully evaded throughout the story. He sees that Maupassant's creativity and passion was the source of his death. The animal in man can take two turns, giving life or bringing death. It is the knowledge of the connection between the two, that inexpressible "portent of truth," that moves forward out of the night and the fog to touch the narrator, thus bringing the author's meditation to its close.

The beauty of the story lies in the precision with which it distinguishes the elements of life and death at the very time that it shows that these cannot be finally distinguished. Summaries of three stories by Maupassant provide counterpoint, going from starkness to gaiety as the story takes an opposite course. The seven-page narrative seems expansive.

It is given a larger dimension by the implied lapse of time between the present of the narrator-author, who sits meditating upon the meaning of his experiences and drawing their spiritual design, and the past of the narrator-actor who plays the dual role of experiencer and the mind's pilgrim to knowledge. The space of the story enlarges, too, as the narrator's sense of the world balloons in the energy of his illusions. But finally the space and time of the story contract as the youthful narrator becomes one with the older narrator in the possession of knowledge.

NOTE

13. The phrase "devouring his own excrement" has been deleted from the 1957 and 1966 editions of Babel's work. It is found in the 1936 edition, the last prepared under Babel's supervision.

—Patricia Carden, *The Art of Isaac Babel*. Ithaca: Cornell University Press, 1972: pp. 206–210.

PETER STINE ON BABEL'S DESPAIR

[Peter Stine is a faculty member at Oakland Community College in Michigan, where he is the chief editor of *Witness*, a literary journal. His articles have appeared in *Modern Fiction Studies*, *The Cambridge Quarterly*, *Contemporary Literature*, *Conradiana*, and *The South Atlantic Quarterly*, and he has edited the books *The Sixties* and *Sports in America*.]

We might wonder whether, in addition to the obvious causes, Babel's silence wasn't part of a recognition that his own writing, with its truth-telling depths, could now only propagate despair.

This is suggested in "Guy de Maupassant," a brilliant summary of Babel's spiritual odyssey. Once again the place is Petrograd, 1916, with himself as a young Bohemian writer, spending his mornings "hanging around the morgues and police stations" (*CS*, p. 329), his evenings dismissing Tolstoy's conversion to religion as "yellow .... all fear" (*CS*, p. 372), abiding by the wisdom of his ancestors that "we are born to enjoy our work, our fights, and our love; we are born for that and for nothing else" (*CS*, p. 329). Adrift in this callow buoyancy, Babel finds work in assisting the translations of Raisa, a handsome Jewess whose wizened husband has grown rich selling war materials to the army. Soon Raisa ravishes his dreams. He woos her with his mastery of Maupassant until one night, with both of them drunk, he reads aloud "L'Aveu," and their identities merge into their fictional counterparts: the lascivious Polyte and modestly submissive Céleste. After the seduction ("Of all the gods ever put on the crucifix, this was the most ravishing" [*CS*, p. 336]), Babel feels intoxicated with life; yet returning to his digs he finds a biography of Maupassant and reads through the night:

> That night I learned from Edouard Maynial that Maupassant .... was twenty-five when he was first attacked by congenital syphilis. His productivity and *joie de vivre* withstood the onsets of the disease. At first he suffered from headaches and fits of hypochondria. Then the specter of blindness arose before him. His sight weakened. He became suspicious of everyone, unsociable and pettily quarrelsome. He struggled furiously, dashed about the Mediterranean in a yacht, fled to Tunis, Morocco, Central Africa .... and wrote ceaselessly. He attained fame, and at forty years of age cut his throat; lost a great deal of blood, yet lived through it. He was then put away in a madhouse. There he crawled about on his hands and knees, devouring his own excrement. The last line in his hospital report read: *Monsieur de Maupassant va s'animaliser*. He died at the age of forty–two, his mother surviving him. (*CS*, pp. 337–338)

Now Babel senses that although appropriating Maupassant's techniques of irony, he had missed his mentor's tragic sense, as he had Tolstoy's and Raisa's earlier. "The fog came close to the window, the world was hidden from me. My heart contracted as the foreboding of some essential truth touched me with light fingers" (CS, p. 338). Fifteen years of experience had lifted the fog for the composer of these lines and confirmed their sense of personal foreboding. Like Maupassant, he would die of an "incurable ailment" in his early forties, his mother surviving him.[39]

NOTE

39. Babel's "incurable ailment," of course, was not syphilis, but its moral equivalent, the allure of violence, which, he acknowledged, found its natural expression in his headaches, asthma, and generally poor health.

—Peter Stine, "Isaac Babel and Violence." *Modern Fiction Studies* 30, no. 2 (1984): p. 254.

CHARLES ROUGLE ON THE FUSION OF ART AND REALITY

[Charles Rougle is Professor of Slavic Languages and Literature at the State University of New York in Albany. Notably, he translated Alexander Bogdanov's *Red Star: The First Bolshevik Utopia.*]

Art and life finally fuse as passion opens the "grave of the human heart":

The night had placed beneath my famished youth a bottle of Muscatel '83 and twenty-nine books, twenty-nine petards charged with pity, genius, passion.... I jumped up, knocked over the chair, bumped the shelf. The twenty-nine volumes crashed to the floor, their pages flew open, they fell on their sides ... and the white nag of my fate set off at a walk. (272)

As he returns home after his apparent conquest we see him reveling in the primordial joy released by this merger of art and eros:

I was sober and could walk a straight line, but it was much better to stagger, and I reeled from side to side, singing along in a language I had just made up. Fog rolled in billows through the tunnels of streets lined by a chain of lamps. Monsters roared behind boiling walls. The roads severed the legs of those who walked along them. (272)

His triumph would seem to be complete—the young self-proclaimed Messiah of joyous passion in art and life has proved himself a worthy successor to the French master. Or has he? If it is suggested that all the other characters of the story suffer from some real or figurative visual defect, accompanying the narrator's claims to authority there is in fact a growing body of evidence that something is wrong with his youthful vision as well. The first indication of a discrepancy between conceived image and real self occurs immediately upon his initial declaration of his philosophy of life. Although it does not necessarily negate the content of that pronouncement, the use of the word *ratsei* ("harangues," "perorations") to describe his outpourings introduces an unmistakable note of irony (272). The gap widens considerably in a crucial passage exactly halfway through the story. Juxtaposed with another of the narrator's harangues—the attack on Tolstoi—is his erotic dream of the washerwoman Katia. The next morning he comes face to face with her and discovers, not the willing young beauty of his puerile fantasies, but "a wilted woman draped in a shawl, with ash-gray hair and chapped hands" (274). Immediately following this is the story he tells Raisa of his childhood. "To his own amazement" it turns out to be a gloomy tale that presents him not in the role of the passionate, adventurous young artist he has sought to convey thus far, but as a lonely little boy seeking maternal comfort (274).

If his image of himself and his view of the surrounding reality are dubious, similar doubts arise with respect to his interpretation of the model he has chosen to emulate. First of all, for an artist who has made meticulous precision a cornerstone of his aesthetics, in his presentation of Maupassant's stories he takes some rather curious liberties with the originals. Thus in "Idylle" the young man on the train is not a carpenter (*plotnik*, 273) but is quite explicitly a "tiller of the soil" who carries a shovel and pickaxe.[17] The translation of "L'aveu" contains even more prominent such "slips." Céleste pays Polyte ten, not fourteen sous; she wears blue, not red stockings; the hood of the carriage is described quite simply "as of black leather," not brownish or reddish (*poryzhevshii kozyrek*, 276). There are also some additions: Maupassant has nothing about Céleste "moving her skirts" (*otodvinula iubki*), nothing about Polyte drinking calvados (*khvativshii sidra pered ot" ezdom*), nothing about the horse's "lips pink with age" (*rozovye of starosti guby*).

All of these alterations are minor, and taken alone they do not profoundly affect our reading of the story. In the larger context, however, they are indicative of a subjectivity in approach that goes beyond poetic license to become a rather eclectic interpretation of Maupassant himself. Thus any reader familiar with the works treated in the story would certainly agree with James Falen that Babel has selected in the French author, "still another peculiar figure [the first being Gogol] to epitomize his literature of joy,"[18] for the natural exuberance that has caught the narrator's eye in all three tales is ultimately outweighed by a profoundly pessimistic view of human limitations and vices that he chooses to ignore.

In the light of these observations, the narrator's triumphant stagger through the streets of St. Petersburg becomes not a confirmation of his prowess as man and artist, but the climax of solipsistic illusion that, all his insistence on disciplined craftsmanship to the contrary, renders the whole world an extension of his fantasy.[19] It seems quite appropriate, then, that he should find Kazantsev asleep over a copy of Don Quixote[20] when he returns to the garret, for the literary allusion prompts the reflection that it is in fact he who has been playing the part of the romantic dreamer out on a quest for Dulcinea. (...)

This insight can be read on several levels. It is tempting, first of all, to view it as a comment by Babel himself on his own situation as he gazes out into the approaching gloom of Stalinism. As has been noted elsewhere, it also implies the discovery of mortality, suffering, and pain in both life and art and is a tribute to artists such as Maupassant who have courageously battled against them.[21] This realization in turn, however, leads directly to one of the central oppositions in Babel's work as a whole. To extend the metaphor of "Line and Color," at the "color" pole there is the world of the poetic imagination, which in Babel tends strongly toward the vibrantly erotic and sensual, and initially we find the narrator of "Guy de Maupassant" at this end of the spectrum. Perceiving the essence of art to lie in a fusion of the imagination and instinctual, amoral passion, he plays out this role in the seduction. As always, however, the subjective exuberance of "color" runs up against the stringent demands of "line," which on the technical level impose upon the artist rigorous standards of craftsmanship and precision and in a broader sense imply a confrontation with extra-aesthetic, ruthlessly objective reality. Art, we are told by the final lines of "Guy de Maupassant" and the entire oeuvre of Babel upon which they retrospectively comment, emerges from the charged and never fully resolved tension that arises between imagination and fact, life and death, passion and suffering, sensuality and morality. Or, in the key metaphors of Babel's literary manifesto, Babel is describing the moment at which he first realized that his art of sun and sea would forever have to contend with the dark St. Petersburg fogs of anxiety and guilt that pervade the literary tradition of which he in the final analysis is an organic part.

NOTES

17. Guy de Maupassant, *Contes et nouvelles*, I (Paris, 1974), p. 1193.

18. Falen, *Isaac Babel*, n. 19, p. 56.

19. Carden, *The Art of Isaac Babel*, p. 207.

20. Further attention is drawn to the work by mention of the edition (1624) and the dedication on the title page to the Duc de Broglie. It is difficult to determine whether these are minor errors on Babel's part or should be counted among the many other little discrepancies of fact that riddle the story. There is no 1624 edition of *Don Quixote*, and the first Duc de Broglie was born in 1671, long after Cervantes's death. A letter to Gor'kii (*Izbrannoe*, p. 431) contains a mention of a certain Kudriavtsev (Kazantsev's probable real prototype) who owned a copy described as once belonging "to some duke or other."

21. Ehre, p. 124.

—Charles Rougle, "Art and the Artist in Babel's Guy de Maupassant." *The Russian Review* 48, no. 2 (April 1989): 178–79, 180.

[Victor Erlich is Professor Emeritus at Yale University. He has authored a number of studies devoted to the 1920s, including a mongraph on the Formalists, and "Color and Line: Notes on the Art of Isaac Babel" in *Isaac Babel*. Erlich also wrote *Modernism and Revolution: Russian Literature in Transition*.]

In Babel's justly celebrated metaliterary narrative, "Guy de Maupassant" (1932)[4] the relationship between art and reality is more complex than it appeared to the boy narrator of "In the Basement." Seen from the vantage point of its pivotal event—the ultra-literary seduction—the story could be described as a matter of life imitating art. The struggling young writer who serves here as the central consciousness, sets out to assist an alluring and well-heeled young Jewish matron, Raisa Benderskaia, in translating Guy de Maupassant's stories into Russian. She had told the narrator: "Maupassant is the only passion of my life" (II, 218). However, her literary skills are no match for her enthusiasm for the French master. During one of the sessions, the narrator reenacts the current assignment, Maupassant's well known "L'Aveu," by emulating the story's slyly insistent coachman, M. Polyte, who after many a ride finally has his way with the heretofore uncooperative red-haired peasant wench Céleste. Emboldened by the wine conveniently drawn by Raisa from her husband's cellar, the young man finds himself echoing M. Polyte's operative phrase, "And what about having some fun today, *ma belle*?" His fellow translator proves as receptive as was, at long last, the heroine of "L'Aveu."

The sun-drenched eroticism of de Maupassant's story, as read by Babel, seems to provide a fitting text for the narrator's sexual initiation: consummate art of fiction opens the floodgate of sensuality, teaches *joie de vivre*.

Yet the story ends on a vastly different, and more ominous note. Having staggered home through the fog, less intoxicated than feigning intoxication, the narrator begins to read a book on Guy de Maupassant's life and work, only to confront some appalling facts:

He was twenty-five when he was first attacked by congenital syphilis. The fertility and *joie de vivre* contained within him resisted the disease ... he struggled furiously, dashed about the Mediterranean, ... and wrote ceaselessly. Having attained fame, at forty years of age, he cut his throat, lost a great deal of blood, and survived. He was put away in a madhouse. There he crawled on all fours, devouring his own excrement. The last line in the hospital report read: *"M. de Maupassant va s'animaliser."* He died at forty-two. His mother survived him.

I finished the book and got out of bed. The fog came down to the window and concealed the world. My heart contracted. A foreboding of the truth touched me lightly (223).

The fog that conceals the outside world from the narrator may well be a metaphor for the elusiveness of some essential truth, half revealed to him. Whatever the exact nature of this truth, it clearly has to do with the dark underside of what appears as a life-affirming creative accomplishment. Since the phrase "congenital syphilis" suggests an Ibsenian curse, rather than a self-inflicted wound, a dire risk incurred in an unselective search for experience, it would be inaccurate to speak of the inordinate or ineluctable "cost of art." What seems at issue rather is a precarious if not adversarial relationship between a writer's life and his art, with "fertility" or creativity pitted, in an unequal battle, against hereditary and incurable disease. Arguably, the finale of "Guy de Maupassant" brings us back, though in a vastly different context, to the theme sounded "In the Basement"—that of art as a would-be antidote to intolerable actuality. For what is strongly intimated here is a sobering, indeed chilling recognition that where the writer's plight, as well as his or her oeuvre, is attended to, many a pleasure-giving work can be shown to have been created against the backdrop, indeed, in defiance of misery and degradation.

NOTE
4. The story dates from 1920–22.

—Victor Erlich, "Art and Reality: A Note on Isaak Babel's Metaliterary Narratives," *Canadian Slavonic Papers* 36, nos. 1–2 (March-June 1994): pp. 109–110.

ALEXANDER ZHOLKOVSKY ON TOLSTOY ALLUSIONS

[Alexander Zholkovsky is Professor of Slavic Languages and Literatures at the University of Southern California. His books include *Bluzhdaiushchie sny I drugie raboty* and *Text Counter Text: Rereadings in Russian Literary History*.]

The "father-and-son combat" is also a recurrent theme in Babel'. But, where Tolstoy's and Turgenev's "Oedipi" suffer passively, Babel''s are more aggressive. They

? secretly, under a *skaz* disguise, relish the retaliatory torture visited upon the "fathers";[24] or

? more openly, although still detachedly, admire the masters of the whip (e.g. D'iakov); or even

? admit envying them ("The Death of Dolgushov") and aspire, in accordance with the famous nietzschean maxim, to wield the whip themselves, a feat in which they occasionally succeed (e.g. in "My First Goose," with "someone else's sword" instead of the whip; 1960: 75).

In "Maupassant" the motif of "body writing"—writing on the body of a father, son, woman—is present, but only figuratively: the weapon taken up by the hero in his battle for the mother figure (Raisa) is an "iron period" symbolizing his literary power. The story's bottom line on "life-creating supermanism," too, is rather skeptical: the closing pantomime is painfully far from triumphal. And yet, one cannot help being struck by the textual kinship of the well timed period chillingly entering the human heart and the swishing of the whip whose supple leather body instantaneously bites into that of the young reader of Turgenev. (...)

Babel' maximized the inherent contradictions in Tolstoy's themes of clothing, naked body, nonverbalism, pantomimes and violence, thereby changing the ideological equation. For him, art was not a quest for but rather the creation of Truth, not the baring of reality, but its transformation. The archetypal challenge for the artist is not the tabooed naked body but its need for galvanization by an aesthetic miracle. The way out is not in renouncing life (family, military service, worldly interests or even biological existence itself) but in creatively mastering it (in particular, a woman's soul and body) through an artistic word-deed in which silent body movements often predominate. This aesthetic action may be violent, even armed: at issue is not its immorality, only its success—that is, its "how" rather than its "what," after all.

And the inclusion of Tolstoy in "Maupassant" is not accidental. Maupassant's death, which crowns the story's plot, occurred on 6 July 1893, antedating by a year Babel's birth (13 July 1894) and the appearance of Tolstoy's "Foreword to the Works of Guy de Maupassant" (1894; hereafter "Foreword").[31] Babel's obsession with both authors makes his unfamiliarity with "Foreword" highly improbable. In fact, the critical gauntlet thrown down to Maupassant by Tolstoy and picked up by Babel', as well as some textual correspondences, make "Foreword" a likely subtext of "Maupassant," especially of its finale:

He was twenty-five when he was first attacked by congenital syphilis. His productivity and *joie de vivre* resisted the onsets of the disease.... He struggled furiously, dashed about the Mediterranean in a yacht ... and wrote ceaselessly. He attained fame ... cut his throat, lost a great deal of blood, yet lived through it. He was then put away in a mad-house. There he crawled about on his fours, devouring his own excrement. The last line in his hospital report read: *Monsieur de Maupassant va s'animaliser* ("Monsieur de Maupassant has turned into an animal"). He died at the age of forty-two ... A foreboding of truth touched me [*Predvestie istiny kosnulos' menia*] (1960: 337–38).

NOTES

24. "And he began to whip [*pletit*] Dad..." ("A Letter," 1960: 50); "Then I ... trampled on him for an hour or maybe more" ("The Life and Adventures ...," 1960: 106).

31. Remarkably, this "Foreword" ("Predislovie k sochineniiam Giui de Mopassana") has been translated into English as "Guy de Maupassant," L. N. Tolstoi, *The Novels and Other Works: Essays, Letters, Miscellanies* (New York: Charles Scribner's Sons, 1907), 2:161–81.

—Alexander Zholkovsky, "How a Russian Maupassant Was Made in Odessa and Yasnaya Polyana: Isaak Babel and the Tolstoy Legacy." *Slavic Review* 53, no. 3 (Fall 1994): p. 679, 682.

WORKS BY
Isaac Babel

(original Russian publications)

Rasskazy, 1925.

Liubka Kazak. Rasskazy, 1925.

Rasskazy, 1925.

Istoriia moei golubiatni—Rasskazy, 1926.

Konarmiia, 1926.

Benia Krik: Kino-Povest', 1926.

Bluzhdaiushchie zvezdy, 1926.

Rasskazy, 1927.

Zakat, 1928.

Odesskie rasskazy, 1931.

Rasskazy, 1932.

Rasskazy, 1934.

Mariia, 1935.

Rasskazy, 1936.

Izbrannoe, 1957.

Izbrannoe, 1966.

Izbrannoe, 1966.

Konarmiia. Odesskie rasskazy. 1991.

Likuia I sodrogaias'; Rasskazy I p'esny raznykh let; Odesskie rasskazy, 1992.

Petrogradskaia proza, 1993.

Izbrannoe, 1996.

Translations in English

Red Cavalry, 1929.

Benia Krik, A Film-Novel, 1935.

Benya Krik, the Gangster and Other Stories, 1948.

Collected Stories, 1955.

Sunset, (a play) 1960.

Liubka the Cossack and Other Stories, 1963.

Isaac Babel: The Lonely Years 1925–1939: Unpublished Stories and Private Correspondence, 1964.

Marya, 1965.

You Must Know Everything: Stories 1915–1937, 1969.

The Forgotten Prose, 1978.

Petersburg 1918, 1989.

Collected Stories, 1994.

1920 Diary, 1995.

The Complete Works of Isaac Babel, 2002.

Isaac Babel

Andrew, Joe. "Babel's 'My First Goose." *In the Structural Analysis of Russian Narrative Fiction*. Staffordshire: Keele University, 1984.

Avins, Carol J. "Kinship and Concealment in *Red Cavalry* and Isaac Babel's 1920 Diary." *Slavic Review* 53, no. 3 (Fall 1994): 694–709.

Bar-Yosef, Hamutal. "On Isaac Babel's 'The Story of My Dovecot.'" *Prooftexts: A Journal of Jewish Literary History* 6, no. 3 (September 1986): 264–71.

Bloom, Harold, ed. *Isaac Babel*. New York: Chelsea House Publishers, 1987.

Brown, Edward J. "Isaac Babel: Horror in a Minor Key." *Russian Literature Since the Revolution*, New York: Collier, 1963, 115–124.

Carden, Patricia. *The Art of Isaac Babel*. Ithaca: Cornell University Press, 1972.

Danow, David K. "The Paradox of *Red Cavalry*." *Canadian Slavonic Papers* 36, nos. 1–2 (March–June 1984): 43–54.

———. "A Poetics of Inversion: The Non-Dialogic Aspect in Isaac Babel's *Red Cavalry*." *Modern Language Review* 86, no. 4 (1991): 937–53.

Ehre, Milton. "Babel's *Red Cavalry*: Epic and Pathos, History and Culture." *Red Cavalry: A Critical Companion*, edited by Charles Rougle. Evanston, IL: Northwestern University Press, 1996.

———. *Isaac Babel*. Boston: Twayne, 1986.

Erlich, Victor. "Art and Reality: A Note on Isaak Babel's Metaliterary Narratives." *Canadian Slavonic Papers* 36, nos. 1–2 (March–June 1984): 107–114.

———."Color and Line: The Art of Isaac Babel." *Modernism and Revolution*. Cambridge: Harvard University Press, 1994.

Falchikov, M. "Conflict and Contrast in Isaak Babel's *Konarmiya*." *Modern Language Review* 72, no. 1 (1977): 125–33.

Falen, James. *Isaac Babel: Russian Master of the Short Story*. Knoxville: University of Tennessee, 1974.

Gereben, Agnes. "The Writer's Ego in the Composition of Short Stories." *Essays in Poetics* 9, no. 1 (1984): 38–77.

Hetenyi, Zsuzsa. "The Visible Idea: Babel's Modelling Imagery." *Canadian Slavonic Papers* 36, nos. 1–2 (March–June 1984): 55–68.

Hyman, S. "Identities of Isaac Babel." *Hudson Review* 8, no. 4 (1956): 149–52.

Iribarne, Louis. "Babel's *Red Cavalry* as a Baroque Novel." *Contemporary Literature* 14, no. 1 (1973): 58–77.

Klotz, Martin B. "Poetry of the Present: Isaac Babel's *Red Cavalry*." *Slavic and East European Journal* 18, no. 2 (1974): 160–69.

Kornblatt, Judith. "Isaac Babel and His Red Cavalry Cossacks." *The Cossack Hero in Russian Literature: A Study in Cultural Mythology*. Madison: University of Wisconsin Press, 1992.

Lee, Alice. "Epiphany in Babel's *Red Cavalry*." *Russian Literature Triquarterly* 2 (1972): 249–60.

Lowe, David. "A Generic Approach to Babel's *Red Cavalry*." *Modern Fiction Studies* 28, no. 1 (1982): 69–78.

Luplow, Carol. "Paradox and the Search for Value in Babel's *Red Cavalry*." *Red Cavalry: A Critical Companion*, edited by Charles Rougle. Evanston, IL: Northwestern University Press, 1996.

Marder, H. "The Revolutionary Art of Babel." *Novel* 7 (1973–74): 54–61.

Mendelson, Danuta. *Metaphor in Babel's Short Stories*. Ann Arbor: Ardis Publishers, 1982.

Murphy, A. B. "The Style of Isaak Babel." *Slavonic and East European Review* 44 (1966): 361–80.

Nakhimovsky, Alice Stone. "Isaac Babel." *Russian-Jewish Literature and Identity*. Baltimore: John Hopkins University Press, 1992.

Pirozhkova, A. N. *At His Side: The Last Years of Isaac Babel* trans Anne Frydman and Robert L. Busch. South Royalton, VT: Steerforth Press, 1996.

Reid, Alan. "Isaak Babel's *Konarmiia*: Meanings and Endings." *Canadian Slavonic Papers* 33, no. 2 (June 1991): 139–50.

Poggioli, Renato. "Isaac Babel in Retrospect." *The Phoenix and the Spider*. Cambridge: Harvard University Press, 1957.

Rosenthal, Raymond. "The Fate of Isaak Babel." *Commentary* 2 (1947): 126–31.

Rougle, Charles. *Red Cavalry: A Critical Companion.* Evanston, IL: Northwestern University Press, 1996.

Schreurs, Marc. "Procedures of Montage in Isaak Babel's *Red Cavalry.*" *Studies in Slavic Literature and Poetics* 15. Amsterdam: Rodopi, 1989.

Shcheglov, Yuri K. "Some Themes and Archetypes in Babel's *Red Cavalry.*" *Slavic Review*, 53, no. 3 (Fall 1994): 653–70.

Sicher, Efraim. "The Duality of the Alienated Jewish Narrator in Modern Jewish Literature: An Analysis of Semiotic Modelling in the Prose of Isaak Babel." *Proceedings of the Eighth World Congress of Jewish Studies*, vol. 3, 129–34. Jerusalem: World Union of Jewish Studies, 1982.

———. "The Jewishness of Babel." *Jews in Russian Literature After the October Revolution: Writers and Artists between Hope and Apostasy.* New York: Cambridge University Press, 1995.

———. "The Jew on Horseback: On the Question of Isaak Babel's Place in Soviet Jewish Literature." *Soviet Jewish Affairs* 13, no. 1 (1984): 37–50.

———. *Style and Structure in the Prose of Isaac Babel.* Columbus, Slavica Publishers, Inc., 1986.

———."The Trials of Isaak: A Brief Life." *Canadian Slavonic Papers* 36, nos. 1–2 (March–June 1984): 7–42.

Stine, Peter. "Isaac Babel and Violence." *Modern Fiction Studies*, 30, no. 2 (1984):237–55.

Terras, Victor. "The Structure of Babel's Short Stories in *Red Cavalry.*" *Red Cavalry: A Critical Companion*, edited by Charles Rougle. Evanston, IL: Northwestern University Press, 1996.

Trilling, Calvin. "Isaac Babel." *Beyond Culture: Essays on Literature and Learning.* New York: Viking Press, 1965.

Van Baak, J. J. "The Function of Nature and Space in *Konarmiia* by I. E. Babel." *Dutch Contributions to the Eighth International Congress of Slavists, Zagreb-Liubliana.* Amsterdam: Benjamins, 1979.

Van der Eng, Jan. "*Red Cavalry*: A Novel of Stories." *Russian Literature* 33 (1993): 249–64.

Williams, Gareth. "The Rhetoric of Revolution in Babel's *Konarmija*." *Russian Literature* 15, no. 3 (1984): 279–98.

Young, Richard. "Theme in Fictional Literature: A Way into Complexity." *Language and Style* 13, no. 3 (1980): 61–71.

Zholkovsky, Alexander. "Isaak Babel, Author of Guy de Maupassant." *Canadian Slavonic Papers* 36, nos. 1–2 (March–June 1984): 89–106.

ACKNOWLEDGMENTS

The Art of Isaac Babel by Patricia Carden. Ithaca, Cornell University Press, 1972. © 1972 by Cornell University Press. Used by permission of the publisher, Cornell University Press.

"Poetry of the Present: Isaac Babel's *Red Cavalry*" by Martin B. Klotz. From *Slavic and East European Journal* 18, no. 2 (1974). © 1974 by AATSEEL. Reprinted by permission.

"Babel's 'My First Goose'" by Joe Andrew. From *The Structural Analysis of Russian Narrative Fiction*. Staffordshire: Keele University, 1984. © 1984 by Keele University. Reprinted by permission.

"Isaac Babel and Violence" by Peter Stine. From *Modern Fiction Studies*, 30, no. 2 (1984). © 1984 by Johns Hopkins University Press. Reprinted by permission of the publisher.

Style and Structure in the Prose of Isaak Babel by Efraim Sicher. Columbus: Slavica, 1985. © 1985 by Efraim Sicher. Revised especially for this volume. Reprinted by permission of the author.

"Some Themes and Archetypes in Babel's Red Cavalry" by Yuri Shcheglov. From *Slavic Review* 53, no. 3 (Fall 1994). © 1994 by American Association for the Advancement of Slavic Studies, Inc. Reprinted by permission.

"On Isaac Babel's 'The Story of My Dovecot'" by Hamutal Bar-Yosef. From *Prooftexts* 6, no. 3 (September 1986). © 1986 by Hamutal Bar-Yosef. Reprinted with permission of the author.

"Isaac Babel." In *Russian-Jewish Literature and Identity* by Alice Stone Nakhimovsky. Baltimore: John Hopkins University Press, 1991. © 1991 by Johns Hopkins University Press. Reprinted with permission of the Johns Hopkins University Press.

INDEX OF
Themes and Ideas